The Discovery of California

THE DISCOVERY
OF CALIFORNIA

John Upton Terrell

With drawings by W. K. Plummer

Harcourt, Brace & World, Inc. / New York

Curriculum-Related Books are relevant
to current interests of young people
and to topics in the school curriculum.

To Donna—

my California discovery

Contents

List of Maps

The Discovery of California

1

The
Northern Mystery

IN AUGUST 1540, THREE SMALL
Spanish vessels were stopped by shallow waters and strong
currents near the head of the sea of Cortez, which later would
be called the Gulf of California. On three sides of them
rugged desert coasts swept against the sky in weird formations.
Rising above saffron mesas and tortured ashen washes were
barren red mountains that tumbled away until they were lost
in the haze of illimitable distance. Directly ahead, to the
north, the Gulf was barricaded by networks of frothing shoals.

The pilots and seamen wanted to turn homeward, but the
commander of the little squadron refused and ordered the anchors dropped. He was Hernando de Alarcón, a young, ambi-
tious, and adventurous captain in the service of the Viceroy of
New Spain, Antonio de Mendoza. Although, through no fault
of his own, he would not succeed in completing the perilous
mission on which Mendoza had sent him, he would accom-
plish a feat of great significance, not only to his own country
but to the world.

No foreigner had penetrated the land Alarcón could see before him, and only one other explorer had gone as far up the

Gulf of California. A year earlier, Francisco de Ulloa, who was employed by the famed *conquistador* Hernando Cortez, had sailed northward until he had come upon "water white, like river water." Late one afternoon in September 1539, Ulloa had anchored his two ships for the night in a channel near Gore Island.* So powerful were the tidal currents that he thought them "marvelous." When the next day dawned, "it being low tide, we saw the whole sea where we must pass, between one land and the other, closed by shoals."

Ulloa had found the raging waters pouring from the delta of the Colorado River of the West, a mighty stream not then known to exist. Believing the reefs ahead to be impassable, he had turned back. He rounded Cabo San Lucas, the southernmost cape of Baja California, and beat his way for several hundred miles up the open Pacific against winter storms before returning to Mexico. In his voyage of two thousand miles Ulloa had proved that Baja California was not a chain of islands, as it was then believed to be, but an unbroken peninsula, and he had put on the map for the first time the long Gulf of California.

Now Alarcón was faced with the same dilemma Ulloa had known at Gore Island—either attempt to find a passage through the formidable shoals or turn homeward.

The expedition with which Alarcón had been entrusted was an essential unit of Mendoza's campaign to conquer the unexplored regions, rumored to contain fabulous treasures, lying immediately north of Mexico. More than two months before Alarcón had left Acapulco, the grand and powerful army of Francisco Vásquez de Coronado had started northward on the

---

* Modern place names are used throughout this narrative.

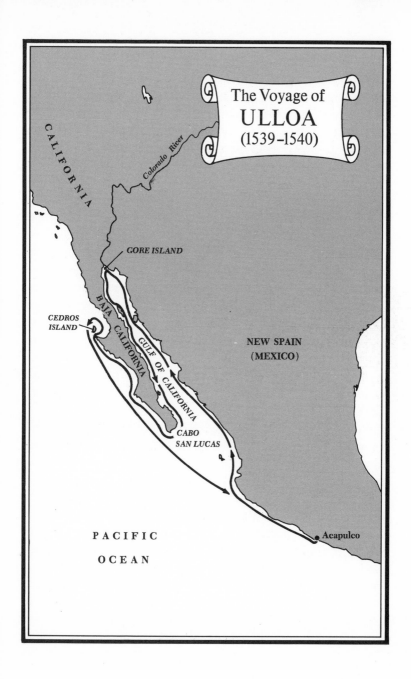

The Voyage of
ULLOA
(1539–1540)

CALIFORNIA

Colorado River

GORE ISLAND

CEDROS
ISLAND

BAJA CALIFORNIA

GULF OF CALIFORNIA

NEW SPAIN
(MEXICO)

CABO
SAN LUCAS

PACIFIC

OCEAN

Acapulco

ancient Indian trade trail that ran along the western coast of
Mexico. On the right of Coronado's long column stood the
great wall of the Sierra Madre, tier after tier and peak after
peak lifting their immensity in awesome heights to the blue
sky, and on the left the shimmering Pacific reached westward,
no one knew how far.

The color of the pageantry rivaled the glory of the dream
that dominated the thoughts of Coronado, the gentlemen ad-
venturers, the soldiers, the red and black slaves struggling
slowly along the rough trail. In the visions of all, the land
ahead surely would be another Peru, where inconceivable
wealth in gold, silver, and jewels awaited them in the Seven
Cities of Cibola, the seven richest cities in the world.

That the Province of Cibola existed there could be no
doubt. Indians who had visited it had spoken of its wonders.
In 1536 Cabeza de Vaca and his three companions, the first
Europeans to cross the continent north of Mexico, had met
Indians who talked of great walled towns and rich mines.
Then Mendoza had sent Fray Marcos of Nice and Estevanico
the Black to verify these reports. The intrepid black, who had
been with Cabeza de Vaca, was commanded by Mendoza to
obey Fray Marcos, but he had ignored the order and had gone
ahead of the padre. Adorned with feathers, strings of turquoise
and tinkling bells, with greyhounds trotting by his side and
trailed by a crowd of Indians, he had marched on across the
deserts to become the true discoverer of lands that one day
would be called Arizona and New Mexico. He had reached
Hawikuh, the westernmost of the Seven Cities of Cibola, but
he had not lived to recount his adventure to the Viceroy.

In Hawikuh (Zuni, New Mexico), Estevanico had been
killed because he told the people that white Christians "were
following him, sent by a great lord, who knew about things in
the sky, and how these were coming to instruct them in divine

Estevanico, wearing feathers, bells, and strings of turquoise, marched across the desert to Hawikuh.

matters . . ." This statement made the people of Hawikuh "think that he must be a spy or a guide from some nations who wished to come and conquer them, because it seemed to them unreasonable to say that the people were white in the country from which he came and that he was sent by them, he being black. Besides . . . they thought it was hard of him to ask them for turquoises and women . . ."

Fray Marcos had not reached Cibola. When Indians brought the news of Estevanico's death down the trail to him, he had turned about and had fled back to Mexico with, as he said, "more fear than food." Yet he claimed that he had seen Hawikuh from a distant hill and that it was larger than Mexico City.

Mendoza suspected the padre of being a victim of his own imagination, and sent the veteran frontiersman, Melchior Díaz, to check on Fray Marcos's story. Winter kept Díaz and his men, who took the first horses into American territory, from reaching Cibola, but they went far enough to confirm that Estevanico had been killed. Although they could learn nothing of treasures in the Land of Turquoises and the Seven Cities, that, of course, did not mean that the treasures were not to be found there. At the time, no one in Mexico could have been convinced that the mountains of Cibola were not made of pure gold.

Lack of geographical knowledge was a handicap under which Viceroy Mendoza labored no less than any other learned man with whom he might have consulted. He formed his plan of conquest with all practicality possible under the circumstances. At Colima he discussed with Coronado his intention to send vessels under the command of Alarcón up the Gulf of California for a twofold purpose. The sea expedition would carry supplies for Coronado's land forces and would conduct explorations beyond the point reached by Ulloa. Perhaps the river Ulloa had discovered would turn out to be a feasible water route to Cibola. Perhaps it might be the best approach to China, or would lead to other rich undiscovered countries in the mysterious north.

Equipment and supply problems prevented Alarcón from starting on schedule. Not until the ninth of May did two of his ships—the *San Pedro*, which was his flagship, and the *Santa Catalina*—make their way out of the beautiful harbor of Acapulco and turn their prows to the north. They would be joined by his third vessel, the little *San Gabriel*, at Culiacán. The start was made, therefore, more than sixty days after Coronado had left on the march to Cibola.

Garbed in splendid silks and linens, his magnificent black beard catching the breeze, his sword gleaming in the sunlight, Alarcón presented an imposing picture on the bridge of the *San Pedro*. He was a man of good nature, a humorist, a braggart and vain about his personal appearance. He had brought with him a favorite greyhound, which trotted dutifully at his heels. He enjoyed pomp and ceremony, and among the crew were a drummer and a fifer. His meals were served to him in his private quarters on silver dishes.

Both the *San Pedro* and the *Santa Catalina* were heavily loaded and well armed. Besides the cannon aboard, the sailors were equipped with swords, shields, helmets, and firearms. In the holds were cargoes of beans, wheat, and ample supplies of other foodstuffs, including crates of live cocks and hens. Alarcón also had taken along a supply of goods such as beads, cords of various hues, and brightly colored cloth, to be used as gifts for Indians.

Shortly after putting Acapulco behind them, they ran into a severe storm. The crew of the *Santa Catalina*, thinking their ship was in danger of sinking, had lightened it by throwing

overboard nine cannon, two anchors, cables, and other indis-
pensible equipment. Both vessels were damaged in the tempest, and Alarcón put into Santiago, on Manzanillo Bay, to
make repairs, obtain additional stores, and re-equip the *Santa
Catalina.*

The next stop was at the port of Guayaval, near Culiacán,
where the *San Gabriel,* loaded with supplies for Coronado,
was waiting. As the squadron continued northward, it kept as
close as possible to the coast, watching day and night for some
signal from the Coronado expedition. They saw none.

Week after week they maintained a constant vigilance—in
vain. Many months later it would be learned that misfortune
and geography were both responsible for preventing the junction of the two expeditions. Scouts from the Coronado army
had been sent to the coast in the hope of obtaining news of the
supply ships. They had learned nothing of them. Indians with
whom they talked reported seeing sails moving northward, but
the identity of the vessels could not be ascertained. Coronado
did not know when Alarcón had started, and therefore had no
means of estimating his possible progress. After passing Pueblo
de los Corazones, an Opata Indian settlement near the present
town of Ures, Sonora, Coronado's route took him each day
farther from the coast. By the time he had reached Hawikuh
in Cibola, the two companies were separated by an airline distance of five hundred miles, and a much greater distance by
the twisting trails on which palatable water was to be found in
the southwestern deserts.

On August 26, 1540, Alarcón reached the point where Ulloa
had turned back, and anchored his three battered vessels—on
the edge of geographical darkness.

Ahead were the white-water shoals, but Alarcón had no intention of accepting defeat as Ulloa had done. The bars and
reefs, he would write later to Mendoza, were so "dangerous

The Voyage of
ALARCÓN
(1540)

CALIFORNIA

Colorado River

CIBOLA

• Hawikuh
(Zuni)

Gila River

•Yuma

• Pueblo de los Corazones

NEW SPAIN
(MEXICO)

BAJA CALIFORNIA

GULF OF CALIFORNIA

Guayaval
• Culiacán

PACIFIC
OCEAN

• Santiago

*MANZANILLO
BAY*

• Acapulco

▲ Probable point reached on first trip.

and forbidding that it was temerity to venture over them even with small boats . . . but since your Lordship had commanded me to report on the secrets of that Gulf, I was determined, even at the risk of losing the ships, not to fail, under any pretext, to reach its end."

Other reasons also influenced Alarcón's decision to proceed. He had no knowledge of Coronado's whereabouts. The Viceroy himself had suggested that Ulloa's river might be a feasible way to reach Cibola, the kingdom of the Grand Khan, or even lead to immense treasures in other unknown northern realms. If he, Alarcón, could be the first to solve the Northern Mystery, he, not Coronado, would receive the honors and rewards. His blood raced at the very thought.

He sent Chief Pilot Nicholaas Zamorano and several crewmen ahead in a launch to seek a channel through the shoals with a sounding lead. As the little craft advanced through the rolling waters, the vessels attempted to follow closely behind it. Soon all three of them were grounded. "We were in such danger that many times the deck of the *San Pedro* was under water," said Alarcón. "And had it not been for the miraculous rise of the tide, which had raised the craft, and, as it were, given us a chance to breathe again, all of us would have been drowned."

The *Santa Catalina* and the *San Gabriel*, being considerably smaller than the flagship, floated first, but the *San Pedro* was soon freed as the water continued to rise, and all three "passed forward with much ado, turning our sterns now this way, now that way, to seek and find the channel. And it pleased God that we came to the very bottom of the bay . . . and here we found a mighty river with so furious a current that we could scarcely sail against it."

Alarcón was the first European explorer to enter the mouth of the Colorado River. He christened it *Buena Guía*—Unfailing Guide—taking the words from a motto on Viceroy Mendoza's coat of arms.

He had broken through the delta, which had been built across the head of the Gulf of California through uncountable millenniums by the silt debouched from the Colorado, but his battle with the furious stream was far from ended. Indeed, it had just begun, for now he encountered one of the great phenomena of nature—the tidal bore.

As the tide of the Gulf rose, between twenty and thirty feet, an enormous wave roared up between the converging shores of the river, smashing its way upstream at times as much as thirty miles against the powerful current of the Colorado—a thunderous, cataclysmic collision that made the surrounding country tremble as if shaken by an earthquake. Then, having spent its strength, the sea water retreated with incredible swiftness. As he prepared to ascend the river, Alarcón, of course, was unaware that the tidal bores of the Colorado River were equaled in size and ferocity in few other places in the world. Nor did he know that he had arrived at the time of year when the magnitude of the bores was greatest—just before the September equinox.

His veteran seamen understood, however, that any attempts to move the ships farther upstream would have been an invitation to unnecessary disaster, and now he listened to them. After anchoring the vessels in a protected channel, he equipped two launches with food and supplies and arms, and taking the most experienced crewmen, he set out.

In his report Alarcón stated that on the first day of fighting their way upstream they traveled six leagues, or nearly sixteen miles.* This distance was covered by backbreaking labor in

---

* The Spanish judicial league equaled 2.634 English miles.

terrific desert heat. While some sailors rowed, others struggled along the bank pulling the boats with ropes.

On the second day after leaving the ships, Alarcón and his men encountered Indians for the first time. They ran from their village shouting angrily at the Spaniards and making threatening gestures. Alarcón ordered the launches anchored in midstream and told his men to remain quiet and motionless. More Indians appeared until the excited crowd numbered two hundred and fifty. Many had bows and arrows and appeared ready to attack if the invaders attempted to land.

Alarcón had with him an Indian interpreter who could speak a dialect of the Yuman language, but he could not make himself understood nor could he understand the words shouted by the people on the bank. Alarcón resorted to pantomime, attempting to show that he came in peace. At last he took off his sword and shield and "threw them on the deck of the launch . . . trying to make them understand by this and other signs that I did not want to fight them, and that they should do likewise. I seized a flag, lowered it, and told my men to remain seated. Then, taking some of the things I carried for barter, I called to the natives and offered them as presents. But no one approached to accept them."

The offer, however, seemed to convince the Indians that Alarcón meant no harm. They held a noisy council, during which Alarcón moved his own boat close to the shore. Presently a warrior emerged, entered the water, and climbed without hesitation into the launch. He carried a staff decorated with shells, which he presented to Alarcón. Alarcón then embraced him, and gave him some beads, and he returned happily to the bank. The Indians dropped their arms, and many of them came forward to receive similar gifts. With the dangerous situation resolved, Alarcón pressed on upstream.

Frequently thereafter the Spaniards sighted Indians. The

boats had advanced about five miles when they saw a large
crowd gathered before another village. They signaled Alarcón
to land, but fearing that he was being lured into an ambush,
he declined and anchored the boats in midstream. There they
spent the night. Alarcón estimated that a thousand Indians
were assembled at the village, and thought that all the men
were armed with bows and arrows. The presence of women
and children, however, indicated that they had no intention of
engaging in a battle with him.

Although Alarcón had no name for these people, his description of them made it clear that he was the first white man
to write of the tall Cocopas, members of the Yuman linguistic family, who dwelt along the lower Colorado almost down
to its mouth. "They were large and well formed, without
being corpulent," he said. "Some have their noses pierced, and
from them hang pendants, while others wear shells. They also
have their ears pierced with many holes, in which they place
shells and beads. All of them [the males], big and little, wear
a multi-colored sash about the waist; and, tied in the middle, a
round bundle of feathers hanging down behind like a tail.
Likewise, on their biceps, they wear a narrow band, wound
around so many times that it has the width of a hand. They
carry small blades of deer bones tied around one arm, with
which they scrape off sweat, and from the other arm reed
canes are hung. They have also a kind of sack tied to the left
arm, using it as an armbag for the bow; and it is filled with
seeds from which they make a sort of beverage. Their bodies
are branded by fire; their hair is banged in front, but in the
back it hangs to the waist. The women go about naked, except
that, tied in front and behind, they wear large bunches of
feathers, colored and glued. They wear their hair like the
men."

Word of Alarcón's arrival evidently had been carried

through the country, for crowds of Indians appeared along the banks at numerous places, waiting for him. After making inquiries by signs and thoughtfully observing their ceremonies and customs, Alarcón concluded that their religion was a form of sun worship. Thereupon, in the hope of ensuring safety for himself and his men, he decided to try an experiment. With the help of his interpreter, he made himself out to be a son of the sun. The ruse was successful. The Indians "stared at me from head to foot, and showed me greater respect than before," he recounted. He was accepted as a supernatural being, and "from then on, whenever they brought me anything they first cast some of it toward the sun, then turned to me and gave me the rest. So I was more respected and better served by them, both in pulling at the ropes and in being supplied with food." Wherever the boats stopped, the Indians "wanted to carry me bodily in their arms to their homes, and did not refuse anything I asked of them." The sailors had little to do except steer the launches, for Indians "took to the ropes so willingly and in such a spirit of rivalry with one another that it was not necessary even to request it of them."

The journey now took on something of the aspect of a pleasure cruise, with obeisance being paid Alarcón wherever he stopped, but he was not at peace with himself. He had been instructed by Viceroy Mendoza to spread the Christian gospel among any pagan peoples he encountered. Instead he was playing the role of a disbeliever, an idol worshiper, and he feared that as punishment his own soul would be relegated to purgatory.

In partial atonement for his sins he made little crosses of sticks and distributed them among the heathens. Yet he dared not reveal their true meaning, for that would have destroyed his own image as son of the sun. The crosses, he told the Indi-

Indians welcomed Alarcón as a son of the sun.

ans, were "symbols of heaven." This delighted them, and they demanded so many crosses that Alarcón and his sailors were unable to make enough to fulfill all the requests. The guilty feeling created by the sacrilegious tricks continued to weigh on Alarcón.

After a week of travel up the river, the interpreter had the good fortune to meet a headman named Naguachato, to whom he could make himself understood. Alarcón persuaded Naguachato to go on with him, and thereafter his communications with the Indians were greatly improved.

The natives asked Alarcón many difficult questions about his descent from the sky to the banks of the Colorado, but he adroitly fended them off and stuck to his role of son of the sun. However, in one settlement he requested the Indians to bring him a log. He made a cross and he and his men knelt before it in prayer. Indians set the cross up in their village, and Alarcón instructed them how to clasp their hands and exhorted them to pray before it each morning at sunrise.

One chief, declared Alarcón, pleaded with him to remain "and be our Lord. Since you do so much good and do not wish to engage us in wars, and since you are a child of the Sun, we wish to serve you always, so we pray you not to go away and leave us."

Alarcón went on, and soon arrived among people whose homes were in mountains to the west but who came to the river each spring to plant crops where there was adequate water to nourish them. They had been informed of his approach, and gave him an enthusiastic welcome. He quoted a leader as crying: "Behold the Master. Let us give him what meat we have, for he is doing good, and has traveled among many discourteous people in order to visit us."

These Indians were Quigyumas, who spoke a dialect of the Yuman language different from the one Alarcón heard farther down the river. Like the Indians who lived permanently along the river, they grew maize, melons, and squashes, and they had cotton plants but did not cultivate the fiber, "for there was no one who knew how to weave."

A Quigyuma elder informed Alarcón that some of his warriors possessed extremely strong shields made from the hide of an animal "with broad feet and forelegs as thick as a man's thigh, the head seven spans long and the forehead three spans wide, eyes as big as fists, and horns the length of a man's shin, with sharp points . . . and it had a short but heavy tail. Raising his arms above his head, he said it was still taller than that."

The description fitted the buffalo, yet the nearest range of that animal was a thousand miles to the east. If Alarcón had ever heard of the American bison, which is extremely doubtful, it is certain that he had never seen one. It is entirely possible, however, that the Quigyuma was talking of shields made of buffalo hide, for long before Alarcón's time Indian trading trails crossed the Southwest from the Pacific Coast to the buffalo plains in Texas. Eastward over them went the beautiful shells of the western sea and the Gulf of California, turquoises, feathers, and cotton products, and westward over them went buffalo hides and robes. Cabeza de Vaca had met Indians in northern Mexico who journeyed each year far to the north of their homes to hunt buffalo.

On September 1, 1540, Alarcón sat in council with Indians who knew of the Province of Cibola. One man said he had been there, and that Hawikuh lay thirty days' travel to the east. That the informant was telling the truth there could be little doubt, for he stated that the chief of Cibola had a dog like the one with Alarcón and ate on dishes like those on Alarcón's launch. The dishes he had seen in Cibola, however, were not the same color as Alarcón's—they were green. Both the plates and the dog, declared the Indian, had been taken from a man whose skin was black.

Alarcón had heard of Estevanico the Black, and he was excited as he moved on up the river. He soon had more news of the daring Estevanico. This time it came from a chief, named Old Man. He, too, had been to Cibola. The Negro who had appeared in Hawikuh had worn small tinkling bells on his legs and arms. The Cibolans had killed him and had cut him in little pieces. The bits of flesh and bones had been distributed among many persons "to show that the Negro was not a god but was only an ordinary man."

Alarcón soon discovered that Indians from the Colorado—probably traders—traveled frequently to Cibola, and that communications between the two widely separated regions were maintained with regularity. On September 6, he reached the territory inhabited by a tribe to whom he gave the name Coana. These people told him of Coronado's arrival in Cibola, an event that had taken place less than two months earlier.

The Coanas were unfriendly, and for understandable reasons. Coronado had slaughtered the Cibolans. Now before them were similar men with beards, wearing armor and carrying firearms. A Coana warrior shouted that Alarcón and his sailors should be put to death before they killed the people of the Colorado River.

The influence and oratory of Old Man prevented violence. "This man is the son of the Sun," said Old Man, "and is our lord. He is doing good; he does not enter our houses even when we invite him; he does not take anything away from us; and he does not molest our women."

With more peaceful relations assured, Alarcón broached the matter of sending couriers to Coronado. He called for volunteers and announced that he would liberally reward any of his men who would make the journey. Only a Negro slave offered to go.

Alarcón then attempted to engage the Coanas to carry a message to Coronado. He met with blunt refusals. Nor would they serve as guides, even if he went himself without any of his men.

The refusal of both sailors and Indians to undertake the dangerous mission was based on the ground that, since Estevanico the Black had been cut up in little pieces and Coronado had slaughtered the Cibolans, it would be foolhardy to venture near the Seven Cities. Certainly the Cibolans would not welcome news of the imminent arrival of more Spaniards. Probably no one would live to reach Coronado. The Coanas added another reason for not going: the trail that must be taken passed through the land of the Cumanas, their deadliest enemies, who dwelt immediately above them along the river. They would be slain if they invaded Cumana territory.

To this Alarcón retorted that Coanas recently had gone to Cibola and had lived to return. In vain he pleaded with Old Man to send warriors with him. "We argued so long over this matter," he wrote, "that he became angry, and the Old Man would have left the boat in a rage, but I restrained and placated him with kind words, because it was very important to retain his friendship. But no matter how attentive I was to him, I was unable to change his mind."

Alarcón had spent twelve days ascending the Colorado River and three days arguing over his proposal to go to Cibola. His food supplies were low. Some of his men were ill. He was not ready to abandon all hope of reaching Coronado, but he decided that any further effort under the circumstances would be futile. He would return to the ships, leave the sick men, take on fresh supplies, come back with a larger force, and renew his attempt to reach Cibola.

Now the question must be asked: How far had Alarcón gone up the Colorado?

Unfortunately, no documentary evidence provides an answer. His descriptions of the country—what few he set down —are too vague to serve as clues. The Indians he encountered inhabited large and poorly defined areas. If he kept a log showing the distances traveled each day, it has never been found.

At the time it was approximately one hundred and fifty miles from the delta of the Colorado to the mouth of the Gila River, but Alarcón said nothing of having found a stream flowing into the Colorado from the east. If he had reached this point, it seems logical to assume that he would have mentioned the confluence, for the trail to Cibola, the old trading trail from the Pacific Coast (the location of which Alarcón had been told) follows the Gila. The trail's crossing of the Colorado was just above the site of the present town of Yuma.

It appears probable, therefore, that Alarcón had ascended the Colorado at this time no more than approximately one hundred and thirty to one hundred and forty miles. The reasonableness of this estimate will be demonstrated by events occurring when he returned to the Coana country.

The Coanas believed that Alarcón was abandoning his quest out of fear. To assure them that he would come back as soon as possible, he left a crewman as a hostage in a Coana village. (As the name of this brave sailor was not recorded, I shall call him El Hombre.)

Alarcón started downstream on either the 10th or the 11th of September. Along the way other Indians pleaded with him to remain with them. "Why are you leaving us?" one chief asked. "What displeasure have you experienced? Did you not say that you would remain . . . and be our master? Turn about, and if anybody does you harm we will accompany you with our warriors and kill him." Repeatedly Alarcón promised that he would soon return.

He had spent twelve days poling, pulling, and rowing against the strong current. Going downstream he reached the ships in less than three days. He found them in good order, the crews well but deeply concerned by his long absence. Quickly he refitted his launches, took aboard goods and supplies, and on September 14, with an able-bodied company, started once more up the Colorado.

The attitude of Indians in villages along the river had changed. Some of them were openly unfriendly, and others acted as if they thought "we were some other people, because we were taking along a fifer and a drummer, and I was dressed differently than when they saw me the first time."

The true reason for the Indians' reactions, as Alarcón would soon learn, was that the news of Coronado's brutality and butchery in Cíbola had spread through all the Colorado River country. Alarcón distributed seeds and showed the villagers how to plant them. He presented the headmen with gifts. "However," he admitted, "I could not induce them to become good friends."

The situation improved when he again reached the Coanas. Old Man welcomed him. El Hombre was not only safe and well but appeared to be extremely happy and enjoying his sojourn. El Hombre's hosts asked that he be permitted to stay with them until Alarcón returned, and El Hombre "remained among them very willingly."

As Alarcón prepared to continue upstream, he had cause to be apprehensive about his safety. Old Man informed him that during his absence some Cumanas had boldly entered Coana country "in search of Christians." Old Man had told them "he knew nothing of any Christians," that the only stranger he had met was a bearded man "called Child of the Sun." The Cumanas had not been persuaded that there was a difference. Christians had conquered and destroyed the people of Cíbola, and they wore beards and armor and carried weapons that roared and spit fire and deadly missiles. The Cumanas implored the Coanas to join them in killing Alarcón and his men, but the Coanas had not agreed. Alarcón quickly made a decision. He sent Coana emissaries ahead to inform the Cumanas that he would visit them. If they wished to be friendly, as he did, well and good. If they wished war he "would give it to them in a way they would not like."*

---

* After they had slain Estevanico, the people of Hawikuh had sent messengers far along the trails to advise other tribes to kill on sight any Christians who appeared. If anyone feared to act, said the people of Hawikuh, they would lend assistance.

Alarcón began to believe that his religious deception, indeed, had been a bad mistake. Nevertheless, he couragously went on up the river, relieved to some extent by Old Man's willingness to accompany him and the unhesitancy with which the Coanas agreed to pull his boats.

Leaving the Coana village in which El Hombre was comfortably ensconced, Alarcón advanced farther than he had traveled on his previous journey.

Now, at last, there is evidence to indicate how far Alarcón went up the Colorado. It is found in his statement that on the second day after leaving El Hombre's village they "came to some very high mountains through which the river flowed in a narrow canyon, where the boats passed with difficulty . . ." They had reached the site of Yuma. Here the Colorado passed in a narrow channel between high cliffs. On their left was the land that would become American California. Alarcón was the first white man to gaze upon it.

As they pushed on, Alarcón wrote, ". . . some Indians came to tell me they were from Cumana, and that among them there was a wizard who wanted to know which way we were going. Upon being told I was coming by the river, he [the wizard, or medicine man] placed some reeds clear across the stream. But we passed over them without suffering any of the harm he thought he would cause us."

Their magic having failed to halt the launches, the Cumanas vanished. Alarcón went on. Once more, to no avail, he sought to induce his own men and the Coanas to go with him to find Coronado. Completely discouraged, he stopped in a Coana village that was the location of Old Man's permanent home, and there he "had a very tall cross erected . . . and on it I carved some letters to indicate that I had come to this place. I did this in order that if people from the general [Coronado] should arrive here they would know about me."

Whether the village in which Old Man lived and in which he erected the cross was on the right or the left bank of the river (that is, in California or Arizona), Alarcón did not record. He did state, however, that it was at this place that he gave up hope of reaching Cibola. "At last," he wrote, "seeing that I could not learn anything I wanted to know, I decided to return to the ships."

More emissaries from the Cumanas arrived to advise him "that their chieftain could not visit him because his country was so far away." Alarcón was no longer interested in the Cumanas. He gave the messengers a small cross for their chief and sent them away, and "Then, on the following day, I sailed down the river."

The Coana village in which Old Man made his home obviously was the northernmost point of Alarcón's journey up the Colorado River. About that there can be no mistake, for his narrative clearly names it as the place where he turned back. The exact site of the village must remain a mystery, but the general vicinity in which it was located can be ascertained from Alarcón's report that only a day's travel downstream was required to reach the town in which he had left El Hombre.

Returning from his first journey up the river, Alarcón had reached his ships in less than three days of riding on the strong current. His descriptions make it certain that on his second trip he had gone above the canyon at Yuma after leaving El Hombre among good friends. A logical estimate of the distance he traveled above Yuma would be forty miles, as it took him only over night to cover the same distance downstream. Therefore, he must have gone above the Gila River, but he made no mention of it.

Somewhere near the river channel where the ships were anchored, Alarcón blazed a tree, carved words on it, and buried letters in a jar in the ground beneath it—a message to tell who-

ever might follow him that he had been there and had done
his best to complete the mission on which Viceroy Mendoza
had sent him. Then he sailed for Mexico.

Despite the vagueness of Alarcón's account, one fact remains indisputable. The land that would become American
California had been reached for the first time, and Alarcón
had been its discoverer.

2

Death
on the Colorado

BY THE LATE SUMMER OF 1540, Coronado's army in Cibola was desperately in need of food supplies, equipment, and ammunition. No word of the fate of Alarcón's relief ships had been received. Coronado had written Viceroy Mendoza of his fear that "they have met some mishap. If they follow the coast, as they said they would . . . and if they have not been overtaken by some misfortune, I maintain my trust in God that they already may have discovered something good, for which their delay may be pardoned."

Coronado could reason that more than sufficient time had elapsed to allow Alarcón to reach the river that flowed into the head of the Gulf of California—unless he had been lost. Perhaps Alarcón was waiting there for some signal from him. Coronado concluded that, whatever the case might be, someone must be sent to make a thorough search for the vessels.

The man he selected for the mission was one of his most trusted and respected aides, Melchior Díaz.

Díaz was born and reared on the frontier of New Spain. Castañeda, chronicler of Coronado's mission, wrote that although he was not a gentleman by birth, he well merited the positions he had held as a government official and a military commander. Astute, intelligent, and capable, he held the rank of captain. He had served as mayor (*alcalde*) of Culiacán, and had endeared himself to Indians in northwestern Mexico by his strenuous efforts to enforce the laws against slavery. He held the confidence of the Viceroy, who had sent him north to verify Fray Marcos' report on the Seven Cities. He, and later Coronado, had found that the padre was an unmitigated liar. Díaz was renowned as both a soldier and pathfinder before he joined Coronado, and he was the most able and experienced frontiersman with the Coronado expedition.

After leaving Cibola with orders to search for Alarcón's ships, Díaz and his small escort reached San Gerónimo de los Corazones, in the Sonora Valley of northern Mexico, late in September 1540. A few days later he started "toward the setting sun" on the perilous quest that would enshrine his name on the roster of the greatest early explorers of the American Southwest—a quest from which he would not return.

If you will spread out a map of northern Mexico, Arizona, and southern California, and if you will ignore all place names and boundary lines and contours on it, you will have before you what Díaz and his men had before their eyes and what knowledge they had of the vast region they were entering—nothing. It was a region in which no white man had ever set foot.

Díaz took with him twenty-five mounted Spaniards, some of them soldiers who had fought under him in Cibola and whose courage and loyalty had been demonstrated. The word *mounted* is especially significant. Díaz had taken the first horses into the western United States in the fall of 1539 on his journey to investigate the death of Estevanico the Black and the stories of Fray Marcos. Now, a year later, the horses of his company were the first to leave their hoofprints on the trail

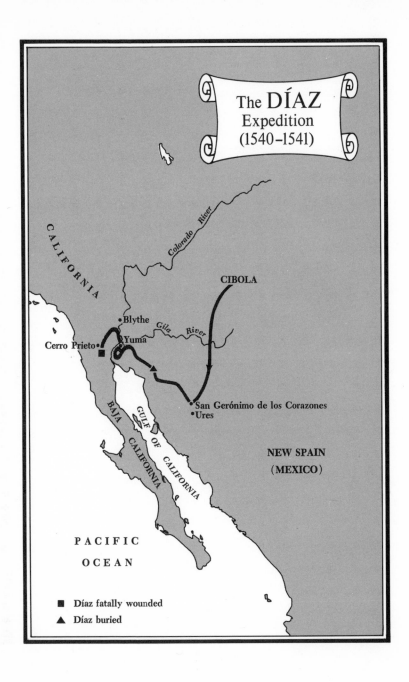

The DÍAZ
Expedition
(1540–1541)

CIBOLA

CALIFORNIA

Colorado River

Blythe
Gila River
Cerro Prieto
Yuma

San Gerónimo de los Corazones
Ures

BAJA CALIFORNIA

GULF OF CALIFORNIA

NEW SPAIN
(MEXICO)

PACIFIC
OCEAN

■ Díaz fatally wounded
▲ Díaz buried

from northern Mexico to the Colorado River, and they would be the first horses to reach the future State of California.

Supplementing Díaz's cavalrymen was a group of Opata Indians from the Sonora Valley, some of whom also had been with him in Cibola. They would serve as packers, camp-tenders, interpreters, and herders of the sheep taken along to ensure a supply of fresh meat. One other animal with the expedition must not be overlooked. It was a greyhound owned by a soldier, and it would play a memorable role in history.

The most important function of the Opatas, however, was to guide Díaz to his goal. The Opatas belong to the large Piman linguistic family, which includes the Papagos, and divisions of these people were spread over immense parts of northern Mexico and Arizona. If Díaz's guides did not know the best route to the Colorado River, they had means of obtaining the needed information, for they had to pass through areas inhabited by Indians who spoke a language similar to their own. Moreover, the Opatas were themselves thoroughly experienced in desert travel.

As far as is known, neither Díaz nor any of his companions made notes as they went along. The reports that have been preserved were written by other chroniclers, such as Castañeda, and they came from the lips of soldiers who had taken part in the great adventure and who had lived to return. While these accounts differ in several essential respects, certain geographical features, mainly the location of water holes known to exist at the time, make it possible to determine the trail that was followed.

Traveling with horses and a band of sheep made it virtually necessary to find adequate supplies of grass and water at regular intervals. Considering this paramount factor, the most feasible route would have been from the vicinity of Ures, Sonora, northwest to Magdalena, westward to Caborca, and north-westward again to Sonoita. Now their course twisted along the present border between Mexico and Arizona, skirting around the northern end of the great Pinacate lava bed. This was the most difficult part of the journey, a section of the terrible desert trail that would come to be known as the Camino del Diablo—the Devil's Highway—and on which many men and animals would perish in the years to come. Near the Tinajas Altas Mountains their route swung northward, probably following the Coyote Wash, until reaching the Gila River near the present community of Wellton. Descending the Gila along the well-traveled ancient Indian trade trail, which came from San Diego Bay on the Pacific coast, Díaz reached the Yuma crossing of the Colorado River.

He was now in the land of Old Man and Naguachato, with whom Alarcón only a few weeks earlier had argued so vehemently about guiding him to Cibola. There is no historical record to show that Díaz met the two chiefs, but whether he did or did not he met their people and gave them reason to be apprehensive. The Indians whom Alarcón had called Coanas heard a strange thunder, a ragged rhythm that was unlike any cadence of the dance drums—the beating of horses' hooves on the desert earth. In Díaz's camps the firelight caught on the sleek sides of the great beasts, from the shadows came the peculiar sounds of their munching on fodder and stamping, and the strange smells of their sweat and their manure filled the air.

Alarcón had arrived by water, and he had shown himself to be a man of peace. Díaz and his men came by land, mounted on prancing animals like those Coronado and his soldiers had ridden when they had conquered and destroyed the Cibolans. The Indians' fear increased when they learned that Díaz, who made no claim to being a son of the sun, had been sent by Coronado to find Alarcón. The Coanas were relieved when

Díaz, his cavalrymen, and the Opatas hurriedly departed after being informed that Alarcón was last seen in the launches several days distant downstream.

Tense with suspense, Díaz and his men rode hard downstream for three days along the left bank of the river, hoping to find the supply ships. If he had started from Yuma, he would have been well into the land of the Cocopas. Alarcón had described the river Indians as "large, and well formed, without being corpulent." Many of the Yuman people stand well over six feet and are extraordinarily powerful. They still reside in the area where Alarcón and Díaz encountered them. The historian Castañeda spoke of them as being "like giants," and wrote that they "are naked and live in large straw cabins built underground like smokehouses, with only the straw roof above ground. They enter these at one end and come out the other. More than a hundred persons, old and young, sleep in one cabin. When they carry anything, they can take a load of more than three or four hundredweight." He recounted how one of these men easily picked up a log that six Spaniards were unable to lift.

Unaware that Alarcón had called the Colorado the Buena Guía, Díaz christened it Río del Tizón, Firebrand River, and Castañeda told why he selected the name. Early mornings in the customarily hot desert country were often very cold, and the Yumans "carry a firebrand with which they warm their hands and body, changing it from one hand to the other as they travel along." Long thereafter the Colorado would be popularly known as the Río del Tizón.

Another early historian related that Díaz was so impressed by the size of these Indians that he wanted to send one to Mexico City, so the Viceroy Mendoza might behold "a man of such magnificent physique." Díaz tried to capture a stalwart young warrior, "but he made such resistance that four Spaniards were unable to bind him, and he yelled so lustily they had to let him go, in order not to indispose the minds of others." Díaz had no wish to start a fight with the Cocopas only for the purpose of entertaining Mendoza.

Presumably on the morning of the fourth day of travel down the left bank, the sharp eyes of the Opatas saw ahead a tree that appeared to have been blazed. With rising hope Díaz pressed his mount forward over the sand. Words took shape as he neared the tree, and when he stopped before it they told that Alarcón had been there and that letters had been buried beside the trunk.

When eager hands had unearthed the jar containing the letters and anxious eyes had scanned them, all Díaz's hope was destroyed. He learned from the letters, wrote Castañeda, "how long Alarcón had waited for news from Coronado's army, and that he had gone back with the ships to New Spain . . ." Alarcón had been unable to proceed farther in his ships, because he had reached the head of the Gulf of California, and "it was explained [in the letters] that California was not an island, but a point of the mainland forming the other side of the Gulf."

Deeply disappointed, Díaz turned back, "without going on to the sea." That is, he did not see the waters of the Gulf of California. The letters reportedly were found about fifteen leagues above the mouth of the river. From this point, Díaz rode upstream "five or six days" looking for "a ford by which to cross to the other side." This journey would have taken him to or above the junction of the Colorado and the Gila.

Now Díaz's actions become mysterious, and give rise to several questions. Knowing Alarcón was gone, why didn't he start back to Cibola to report to Coronado? Why did he want to cross the Colorado to the right bank? What was he hoping to find?

Díaz found letters from Alarcón buried beneath a tree.

At last Díaz found a place where he believed it would be possible to cross the swift river on rafts, and he asked the Indians to supply them. Castañeda told what happened:

The Indians were plotting to attack the Spaniards, and "were waiting for a favorable opportunity." When they were told that "our men wanted to cross, they helped make the rafts with all zeal and diligence, so as to catch them in this way on the water and drown them or else so divide them that they could not help one another."

While the rafts were being constructed, an alert soldier scouting in the adjacent country noticed that a "large number of armed natives" were crossing the river and assembling on a hillside. His suspicions aroused by the scout's report, Díaz had an Indian "captured and locked up secretly in order to question him and learn the truth." The captive claimed to know nothing of any plot to attack the Spaniards, but torture loosened his tongue, and "he told all the arrangements that had been made." This was the plan: "When our men were crossing and part of them had got over and part were on the river and part were waiting to cross, the Indians who were on the rafts should drown those they were helping across and the rest should make an attack on both sides of the river. If they had had as much discretion and courage as they had strength and power, the attempt would have succeeded."

Díaz had the Indian who had confessed killed, and when night came his body, heavily weighted, was thrown into the river. By some unknown means, however, the Indians learned that their strategy had been discovered, and decided not to delay their assault until the crossing was under way.

In the dawn they launched an attack, but Díaz and his men were not caught off guard. As the arrows began to fly, horsemen charged, running down Indians and driving lances through them. Other soldiers and Opatas sent a devastating harquebus fire into crowds of screaming warriors. The attackers were soon routed in disorder, and "had to leave the plain and take to the mountain, until not a man of them was to be seen."

The rafts were made of reeds tied together. They were wide in the middle and pointed at each end. On these buoyant but rickety vessels, Díaz and his men, the sheep, and the lone greyhound crossed the Colorado, "the horses swimming alongside." They had entered California, and the first sheep and horses had been taken into the land that would be called the Golden State.

Regrettably the exact site of Díaz's crossing of the Colorado River cannot be determined from historical records of the time. All that may be said is that it was in the vicinity of the confluence of the Colorado and the Gila. Nor can it be stated with certainty which way Díaz turned after he landed on the California bank. However, the available evidence from old documents is fascinating, even if it is neither irrefutable nor complete, and provides a possible explanation of Díaz's purpose in crossing the Colorado.

In July 1540, a detachment of the Coronado expedition led by Captain Pedro de Tovar had found the Hopi towns in northern Arizona, and there learned of a great river that lay "several days' journey to the west." The Hopis also told Tovar that farther "down the river there were some people with very large bodies." These, of course, would turn out to be the Yumans, whom Alarcón and Díaz would meet on the lower Colorado.

Tovar had no orders to go beyond the Hopi towns, and he rejoined Coronado in Cibola. News of the great river stirred Coronado's curiosity. He asked himself if the river of the Hopis might be the same one that Ulloa had found pouring its wild flood into the Gulf of California, the same river that Alarcón had been sent to explore. In the hope of answering the question, Coronado sent another detachment, commanded by Don García López de Cárdenas, to search for the river.

Cárdenas set out late in August 1540. Passing through the Hopi towns, he and his twenty-five horsemen traveled for twenty days, when they came to a gigantic gorge. They had discovered the Grand Canyon. "They spent three days trying to find a way down to the river . . . The descent was found to be impossible." Cárdenas, too, learned of Indian settlements farther down the river, and he was told of the "people with very large bodies," but Indians warned that impassable deserts lay ahead, and he turned back.

A sixteenth-century historian clearly implied that when Coronado sent Melchior Díaz to search for Alarcón's ships, he instructed him to explore the western area Cárdenas had been unable to reach and to "discover the route" of the river Cárdenas had found. After he had reached the Firebrand River and had investigated its course, said this early account, Díaz had become certain that "it is the river of the grand canyon that Cárdenas saw . . ."

Thus, it is indicated that Díaz traveled far enough up the Colorado to determine that it and Cárdenas' river were one and the same.

Another early historian wrote that after finding Alarcón's letters, Díaz "passed on from the Firebrand River fifty leagues to where he found the country very sandy, windy and filled with large and high sand-banks or dunes . . . which grow, diminish or move depending on the strongness of the wind." Reportedly, Díaz then turned back "for fear of becoming lost." If Díaz traveled this distance up the river from Alarcón's blazed tree, he would have reached a point above Blythe,

California. There are large sand dunes in this area a few miles west of the river.

The only other area of southern California in which immense blowing and moving sand dunes are to be found is between Yuma and the Imperial Valley.* That Díaz skirted them at some time in his wandering in California is an indisputable fact, as proven by the narrative of Casteñada. He wrote that after crossing the Colorado River, Díaz and his company "continued their search for the other coast," meaning the western coast of the Gulf of California. Traveling toward the southwest, "they came upon some beds of burning lava. No one could cross them, for it would be like going into the sea to drown. The ground upon which the Spaniards walked resounded like a kettle-drum, as if there were lakes underneath. It was amazing to see the cinders boil in some places, for it looked like something infernal. They turned away from this place because it seemed to be dangerous and also because of a lack of water."

Díaz may or may not have reached the sand dunes near Blythe, but at least it is known that he passed the sand hills that rise on the eastern rim of the Imperial Valley. From this point he had swung southwestward, and had crossed the present boundary between California and Lower (Baja) California. He continued on this course until he came to the Cerro Prieto (Dark Hill). This place, which "looked like something infernal," is easily identifiable as Volcano Lake, at the foot of Cerro Prieto, about twenty miles southeast of the city of Mexicali. Hot mud bubbles up from ground pots, steam and acrid fumes rise, and wide reaches now known as "rubber meadows" —hot mud covered with an inch or two of soil—tremble and resound as a man walks on them.

---

* The dunes are crossed now by U.S. 80, a four-lane concrete freeway.

Díaz's trailbreakers found firm ground just to the north of Cerro Prieto. After circling the hill, a safe trail continued toward the southwest. They were close to a branch of the Colorado delta known as the Río Hardy. Had they been able to go on they would have traversed a course over which a paved highway now passes between Mexicali and the little village of San Felipe, on the western shore of the Gulf of California.

Their journey ended a short distance below the Cerro Prieto. After he had survived the perils and ordeals of living and exploring for years beyond the farthest frontiers of civilization, fate decreed that Díaz perish as the victim of a freakish accident.

On a day late in December 1540, either the 29th or 30th, the greyhound brought along by one of the soldiers, perhaps being in a playful mood, began to annoy the little band of sheep. The animal ran at the sheep as if it intended to bring one down, scattering them along the trail. Aggravated by this threat to the rapidly diminishing supply of fresh meat, Díaz charged after the dog on his horse and threw his lance at it.

He missed his target, and the lance stuck in the ground immediately before him. Unable to stop his horse quickly enough, "he went over the lance so that it nailed him through the thighs and the iron came out behind, rupturing his bladder." Díaz fell from his saddle and lay writhing and groaning in terrible agony. His men knelt about him, and as he lapsed into unconsciousness they thought him dead.

He was not dead, however, and one account of the tragedy told of his incredible courage and indomitable determination to survive. ". . . he was a man of spirit, and he came to. Seeing there was no one who dared doctor him, he doctored himself." With great effort, Díaz said: "If I only had a silver tube I could get along." He extracted the iron lance, stopped the flow of blood, and bound the wound with cloths.

Díaz's men carried their wounded leader across the desert.

There in the Baja California desert, as the year 1540 neared an end, began one of the most remarkable and brave exploits in all of North American exploration. History does not record a greater display of loyalty and devotion by soldiers for a commander.

Heartsick and despondent, Díaz's men constructed a litter, placed him gently upon it, lifted it to their shoulders, and started for San Gerónimo de los Corazones. If they could have walked the distance in a straight line, they would have had to travel more than three hundred and fifty miles. They had no alternative, however, but to go back northeastward, into California, and follow the trail on which they had come west, a route that would make their journey close to five hundred miles in length.

Indians attacked the Spaniards at the Colorado River, but the harquebusiers drove them off while others got Díaz across on a reed raft. On they marched, hour after hour, day after day, taking turns under the litter, across the Camino del Diablo. When the ground was smooth enough they walked in lock-step, probably with a leader monotonously counting out the cadences, but for countless miles the trail passed through rough land—rock and lava and thick brush, washes and canyons and mesas. In these places they staggered and stumbled under their burden. But they did not give up, and always they moved with all rapidity possible, clinging fervently to the hope that "they would reach the settlements in time for Díaz to be confessed, for there was a priest there . . ."

They lost the race.

Diaz died on January 18, 1541, after living "for about twenty days." Although the date of his death is known, the place is not. All that has come down through history is the simple statement that ". . . the soldiers with great sorrow buried him on a little hill and there erected a cross, covering him with a large mound of earth and stones."

Many persons have searched for the grave of Melchior Díaz. Perhaps it will be found one day, but all records are barren of any clue that might be helpful. The valiant men who carried him for twenty days knew no names for the mountains and deserts they passed, so they had no means of identifying the place in which he was interred—only "a little hill." No one knows how many miles they walked on a given day or how far they would have come in twenty days.

The names of only two of the men who accompanied Díaz have been preserved in documents. They are the soldiers Hernando de Orduna and Pedro de Castro. They were remembered because they carried the sad news of Díaz's death to Coronado in Cibola, and there Castañeda talked with them so that he could give their story to the world.

Too often history recounts only the feats of generals and overlooks, or even forgets, those of their lieutenants. As a consequence, important sights and events are obscured by the histrionics and the shoutings of personages who, enjoying the prerogatives of high office and rank, commanded attention and held the center of the stage.

Of all the brave and able lieutenants who were members of the Coronado expedition, none was more gallant and daring, none was a more able frontiersman, and none accomplished more than Melchior Díaz. He has not been accorded the high place in history he so rightly deserves. Alarcón reached American California when he ascended the Colorado, but he remained on the river. Díaz crossed the Colorado and led his company inland, into American California. Yet, no mountain range, no stream, no desert, no road bears his name. No monument stands to his memory.

3

An Island Grave

IN THE SPRING OF 1542 THE
Viceroy Mendoza had reason to be discouraged. All attempts
to find rich lands north of Mexico had failed. Alarcón had
ascended the Colorado River and had discovered nothing of
value—only more savage Indians and more deserts reaching
away to the horizons. Díaz had broken a trail to the Colorado
only to learn that Alarcón had departed and to die a terrible
death somewhere in the mysterious, worthless country. Coronado was returning from Cibola ill, dispirited, and without
treasure. Moreover, for the past three years Indian uprisings
had kept central Mexico in an almost constant turmoil.

These disappointments and pressing problems might have
caused a man of lesser determination and faith to postpone
further attempts to solve the Northern Mystery and take possession of new countries. That would not have been in keeping
with Mendoza's character. His blood was no less heated by
gold fever than that of any *conquistador*. Furthermore, he believed that somewhere in the north was a water passage, popularly known as the Strait of Anian, through which vessels
could sail from the Atlantic through the land barrier of the

43

continent directly to the Orient. He believed as well that China might be reached by following the Pacific coast northward from Mexico. Mendoza's convictions, like those of most learned men of the time, were indestructible, not to be shaken by the disappointments he had known.

Neither Coronado nor any of the detachments of his army that had been sent out to explore had found the legendary Strait of Anian, but they had heard from Indians tales about large interior waterways. One of these accounts particularly intrigued Mendoza. An Indian to whom Coronado's men had given the nickname of Turk had told them that he was a native of a country in which there was a river two leagues in width. Fish as large as horses swam in this immense stream, and Indians traveled on it in great canoes, with twenty oarsmen on each side. On the prows of these canoes were eagles made of gold. Chiefs sat under awnings on a poop deck while being propelled up and down stream by the rowers.

Another fascinating yarn was being circulated in Europe. A gentleman at the royal court in Flanders reported that he had seen a letter written by Mendoza in which the Viceroy declared that after discovering the Seven Cities of Cibola, Coronado had traveled to the northwest across a great desert and had reached the sea. On the coast Coronado had found ships, presumably manned by Indian sailors, which had sailed for thirty days from their home ports. On the prows of these ships were pelicans made of gold and silver.

This story, of course, was untrue. Coronado did not travel toward the northwest either from the Province of Cibola in New Mexico or, in his later explorations, from the Province of Quivira, which was on the plains of Kansas. Yet, the tale persisted and was published in histories. One historian gave the impression that the Seven Cities and the other Indian pueblos Coronado had visited lay in a line to the northwest instead of to the east and northeast. None of Coronado's men came closer to any sea than the small company led by Melchior Díaz, after it crossed the Colorado at Yuma and rode a short distance into California. Not only the historians, however, accepted the story as fact. For years mapmakers placed both New Mexico and Kansas on the northwest coast of America.

As he analyzed the situation in the spring of 1542, Mendoza obviously was aware that an immense land mass existed directly north of Mexico. That fact had been proven by Coronado, Alarcón, and Díaz. Perhaps the Sea or the Strait of Anian could be reached by traveling directly north or northwest, but that would mean sending another large, extremely costly expedition overland, across the wide deserts known to exist. Moreover, he must have known by this time that the story of Coronado's traveling northwest from the Seven Cities and reaching the sea was false, for he had received reports from Coronado. It is not possible to believe that Coronado would have written untruths to his Viceroy.

Mendoza concluded that the most practical thing to do at the moment was to make another attempt to reach the Orient by sending more ships up the Pacific coast. This was not a new idea, and in spite of the good ships, trained crews, and experienced pilots that were available to Mendoza, there were at least two precedents to support doubts that the venture would be fruitful. Ulloa, in the employ of Cortez, had been defeated in his voyage of 1539–1540, and in September 1541 Mendoza had sent three vessels, commanded by Francisco de Bolanos, to explore the north coast. Bolanos had reached the vicinity of Bahía de Ballenas, on the coast of Baja California, when he was forced to turn back by severe storms, which had badly damaged two of his ships.

Although little is known of the Bolanos expedition and its explorations accomplished nothing, it did achieve a certain historical significance. In the year 1510, ten years before the army of Cortez conquered Mexico and three decades before Bolanos made his unprofitable voyage, a highly imaginative romance of chivalrous adventures was published in Spain. The fanciful story told of a beautiful queen, who ruled over a mythical paradise, and it contained this passage:

> Know ye that on the right hand of the Indies there is an island called California, very near the terrestrial paradise and inhabited by black women without a single man among them and living in the manner of Amazons. They are robust of body, strong and passionate in heart, and of great valor. Their island is one of the most rugged in the world, with bold rocks and crags. Their arms are all of gold, as is the harness of the wild beasts, which, after taming, they ride.

On his return voyage, Bolanos' ships, battered and broken by the terrible storms, found a safe haven and quiet waters in a small bay. Thereafter in official documents the bay was referred to as Puerto de California, a name apparently bestowed on it by Bolanos. When the name California first appeared on maps, a few years later, it was applied to a cape at the southern end of the long peninsula now called Baja California and near the small bay in which Bolanos had found refuge. Therefore, Bolanos is remembered as the mariner who most probably gave the fictional name California to a place that truly existed.

The man Mendoza chose to command the expedition of 1542 was Juan Rodríguez Cabrillo, a Portuguese who had long been in the Spanish service both as a military officer and as a sea captain. Cabrillo had arrived in New Spain in 1520. He had commanded a company of crossbowmen and had taken part in Cortez' campaign against the city of Mexico and in other military actions. Sometime later he had gone with the notorious *conquistador*, Pedro de Alvarado, to conquer Guatemala. He became one of Alvarado's most trusted aides, and was liberally rewarded with farms which provided his family—a wife, two sons, and an unknown number of daughters—with a substantial income.

Because Guatemala was not rich in gold, silver, and precious stones, the conquest was a disappointment to the greedy and irrepressible Alvarado. He constructed a large fleet and in 1540 sailed back to Mexico, seeking new treasure lands to conquer. Cabrillo was second in command of the flotilla.

In Mexico, Alvarado and Mendoza formed a partnership. They concluded plans to send out two strong expeditions. One would seek to discover islands believed to exist in the South Seas and to contain valuable spices and gold. One would explore the northwest (Pacific) coast of New Spain.

Before either of these expeditions had started, Alvarado was killed in an Indian uprising. Mendoza took possession of Alvarado's ships. With some of them Ruy López de Villalobos would cross the Pacific and reach the Philippines. Two vessels of the fleet, the *San Salvador* and the *Victoria*, were assigned to Cabrillo for a voyage of exploration up the northwest coast.

Cabrillo was a skilled mariner and a courageous adventurer, and, as will be seen, the men he selected as his officers were equally capable and intrepid. No detailed log, or full account, of his expedition has been discovered in Spanish archives, but there seems little doubt that one was written by Cabrillo's chief pilot, Bartholomé Ferrer, although it has never been found.

A summary of the voyage prepared by an unidentified author has been preserved, but there are two convincing reasons to believe that Ferrer did not write this brief account. It is written in the third person, hardly a form a man would use in telling of his own personal adventures, and in it the name

Ferrer appears as Ferrelo. It seems reasonable to assume that the pilot would not misspell his own name.*

Customarily, leaders of Spanish expeditions, in addition to exploring new lands, were instructed to plant the seeds of Christianity in the minds of all Indians encountered. Presumably such orders were given to Cabrillo, but no record survives to show that he attempted to obey them, although he was accompanied by a chaplain. He did, however, make every attempt to consult with natives and to maintain peaceful relations with them. He took pains to ascertain their numbers, and he troubled to record the names of many of their villages. These efforts, of course, stemmed from the hope that he would find people who possessed gold and silver, or who could tell him where such treasures were to be found.

Ferrer's statements, cited in the summary of the voyage and in other accounts by early historians, leave no doubt that two other paramount goals were set for Cabrillo in Mendoza's orders. He was to examine the northwest coast to determine if China could be reached by following it, and he was to search for the western mouth of the Strait of Anian.

On Tuesday, June 27, 1542, Cabrillo's two ships stood out from the Mexican port of Navidad, on the border between the States of Jalisco and Colima, into the blue Pacific. The *Victoria* was a tiny open vessel affording little protection for its crew

---

* I think it is important to note that the name has appeared as Ferrelo in numerous modern works, but there is ample documentary evidence to show that the correct spelling is Ferrer. Notable among these authorities is an *Información* prepared in 1560 at the request of Cabrillo's son; an account by the sixteenth-century Spanish historian, Antonio de Herrera, published in 1615; and *Spanish Voyages to the Northwest Coast* by the distinguished historian, Henry R. Wagner, published in 1929 by the California Historical Society.

Cabrillo sailed in well-equipped ships from the port of Navidad.

in rough seas. The *San Salvador*, which was Cabrillo's flagship, was larger, perhaps in excess of one hundred tons. Both were well equipped and their holds contained supplies considered sufficient for a voyage of at least two years.

For more than three days they beat their way north along the Mexican coast.

One writer's account states:

"On Sunday, July 2, [they] had sight of California, having been delayed in crossing [the Gulf of California] almost four days on account of winds which were not very favorable. On Monday, the 3d, they cast anchor at Punta de la California, and remained there two days. From there they went to the Puerto de San Lucas on Thursday and took in [fresh] water, and during this time saw not a single Indian."

Now they were at the southernmost tip of the Baja California peninsula. Here their voyage along the northwest Pacific coast would begin.

Ferrer is quoted as terming "vile" the winds encountered during the next three weeks. On July 25th they anchored in a large bay, to which they gave the name Puerto de Santiago, and Ferrer noted that not far distant were some dangerous reefs called Abreojos. It was in this vicinity that storms had forced Bolanos' damaged ships to turn back. Only Ulloa had gone beyond this point.

August came. On some days they made little or no progress owing to contrary winds. The large island called Cedros by Ulloa, because of cedar trees growing on it, was put behind them on August 10th. Sudden changes in weather frequently occurred, on some days holding them at their anchorages and on other days forcing them to remain at sea. Constantly they watched for Indians, but saw none.

On Monday, August 21, following the coast towards the north and northeast, they "discovered a good port in which they anchored and took in water and wood." On the following day "Captain Juan Rodríguez Cabrillo went ashore and took possession in the name of His Majesty and the most illustrious Don Antonio de Mendoza, naming it 'Puerto de la Posesión.'" Up to this time, although he had landed on numerous occasions, he had not gone through the formality of taking possession of the country. It would have been an unnecessary act, for both Ulloa and Bolanos had preceded him.

They had gone well beyond the farthest north point known to have been reached by Ulloa, although it is not clear how Cabrillo knew this to be certain. The northernmost latitude recorded by Ulloa may have been furnished to him in Navidad or some other Mexican port. Perhaps a map delineating Ulloa's voyage was in his possession. Whatever the case, that he was informed, at least in general terms, of the vicinity in which Ulloa had turned homeward, is indisputable.

At the Puerto de la Posesión "they discovered some Indian fishermen, who at once took flight, but they captured one of them. They turned him loose, however, after giving him some presents, and he went away."

After making needed repairs and dressing sails, on August 27 they left the Isla de la Posesión, slowly working their way along the coast. A few days later, when landing in search of fresh water, they encountered a group of Indians who exhibited no fear and "showed them a spring and a saline which contained much salt." Five of the Indians "who seemed to be intelligent came to the beach. They took them to the ships, and as they went aboard they [the five Indians] pointed out and counted the Spaniards and made signs that they had seen other men who had beards and who had with them dogs, crossbows and swords. The Indians were painted on the thighs, body and arms with white bitumen, put on like slashes in cloth, so that they looked like men in slashed breeches and jackets."

Cabrillo was astounded to hear from these Indians that other Spaniards "were five days journey from there." That could not have been possible. Perhaps the signs of the Indians were misunderstood. Yet there seemed to be no question that they had seen other bearded men and dogs, or, at least, they had heard of them from other natives. They may have heard of Alarcón and Díaz. Most probably they had met Ulloa somewhere along the coast. There were dogs with every expedition, and there had been dogs on Ulloa's ships. Cabrillo did not know what to believe, but he took no chances and gave the Indians "a letter to carry to the Spaniards who they said were inland."

They went on, and now they were heading into total geographical darkness. Now they were gazing at islands and lagoons, bays and estuaries, bare mountains and desert shores never before seen by a European. Now their sails were catching the wind and the salt spray of a sea unknown to men of the civilized world.

September came, and they inched their way northward, fighting fierce currents and strong winds that appeared determined to turn them back. The country improved, and they noted that it was "of reddish color and of good appearance." They began to see trees "like silk-cotton trees except that they are of hard wood." On beaches they found "big thick logs cast up by the sea." They made a landing in a bay on Sunday, September 17, and it was "apparently very good country, there being great savannas and grass like that of Spain." Large herds of antelope dotted the countryside. Once again Cabrillo took possession of the country in the name of his King and his Viceroy. The place now bears the name Ensenada, and if you will look at your map you will see how close they were to the high point of their courageous voyage.

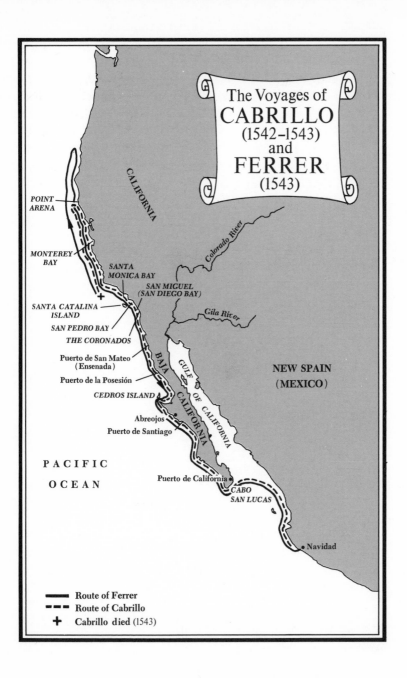

The Voyages of **CABRILLO** (1542–1543) and **FERRER** (1543)

POINT ARENA

CALIFORNIA

Colorado River

MONTEREY BAY

SANTA MONICA BAY

SAN MIGUEL (SAN DIEGO BAY)

SANTA CATALINA ISLAND

SAN PEDRO BAY

THE CORONADOS

Gila River

Puerto de San Mateo (Ensenada)

Puerto de la Posesión

NEW SPAIN (MEXICO)

BAJA CALIFORNIA

GULF OF CALIFORNIA

CEDROS ISLAND

Abreojos

Puerto de Santiago

PACIFIC

OCEAN

Puerto de California

CABO SAN LUCAS

Navidad

— Route of Ferrer
- - - Route of Cabrillo
+ Cabrillo died (1543)

That high point was reached ten days later, although the sailors on the *San Salvador* and the *Victoria* did not think of it in such a way. To them all of these late September days were very much the same. The events of one were seemingly of little more importance than the events of another. For three months they had fought their way northward, marking down bay after bay, island after island, along a forbidding coast that appeared to have no ending.

This is the way the summary recorded one of the great episodes in the history of Pacific Coast explorations:

"Saturday, the 23d, they left the Puerto de San Mateo [Ensenada] and sailed along the coast until the Monday following, making about eighteen leagues and seeing many beautiful valleys, groves of trees and level and broken country.

"On the following Tuesday and Wednesday they sailed along the coast about eight leagues and passed by some three uninhabited islands [the Coronados]. On this day they saw on the mainland some great smokes. [Probably brush fires, which frequently occur on the California coastal hills in the fall.] The country appears good, with large valleys. Inside, there are some high sierras.

"On the Thursday following [September 28, 1542] they sailed about six leagues along a north-northwest coast and discovered a very good closed port . . . which they named San Miguel. After anchoring they went ashore . . ."

Cabrillo had landed in San Diego Bay. He and his men were the first Europeans to reach by sea the land that would become American California.

Now occurred an event which Cabrillo did consider to be of great significance.

When he and his men went ashore "there were some people, three of whom awaited them, while the rest fled. To these some presents were given, and they explained by signs that inland men like the Spaniards had passed, and they displayed much fear." This was the second time that Cabrillo had been told by Indians that Spaniards had been inland from the coast, but on this occasion there was no mystery as to their identification.

"That night," says the summary, "some went ashore from the ships to fish with a net, and it seems that there were some Indians who commenced to shoot arrows at them and wounded three men."

Cabrillo did not order a counterattack. He wanted to establish good relations with these people, to inquire of them about treasure and to learn from them, if possible, whether a great river entered the sea in the area. Also, he had another reason for avoiding a violent clash. He knew the cause of the fear they had shown.

"The following day in the morning they went with the ship's boat farther up into the port, which is large, and brought back two boys who understood nothing by signs; they gave them some shirts and shortly they went away. The following day in the morning [September 30] three large Indians came to the ships and explained by signs that some people like us, that is, bearded, dressed and armed like those on board the vessels, were going about inland. They showed by signs that these carried crossbows and swords; they made gestures with the right arm as if using lances, *and went running about as if they were going on horseback* [italics added], and further showed that these were killing many of the native Indians, and for this reason they were afraid."

If he had guessed it before, as no doubt he had, Cabrillo could now be certain that the Indians of San Diego Bay were telling him of Coronado.

The first people Cabrillo met in territory that would become American California would be given the name of

Diegueños by the Spanish. It was a collective name, being applied to Indians of several small tribes, so it has no ethnic significance. However, most of the people early Spaniards found in extreme southern California were of Yuman stock and were related linguistically to the large tribes of the important Yuman family, which lived on the lower Colorado River and which were discovered by Alarcón and Díaz.

For centuries before the discovery of America, as stated in Chapter 1, Indian trade trails ran from the Pacific coast to the pueblos of New Mexico. Indeed, these trails laced the entire area of the United States. One of the most important and heavily traveled ran from San Diego Bay to the Yuma crossing of the Colorado River. Trade goods passed over this and the other trails, but they were also routes of communication. Alarcón had talked with Indians who told him of the death of Estevanico the Black in Hawikuh, of the invasion by Coronado of the pueblos of Cibola, and of the slaughter of their inhabitants by bearded men who rode horses. The same news had reached the Pacific coast, where it was related to Cabrillo by Indians who feared they would suffer the same fate as the natives of Cibola and those who had fought Díaz on the Colorado River.

The Indians of San Diego Bay need not have feared. Cabrillo had not come there for the purpose of subduing savages, and he did not propose to fight them unless forced to defend himself. This attitude was not what might have been expected of him, for he had served under two great *conquistadores*, Cortez and Alvarado, both of whom were merciless in their treatment of Indian adversaries. Perhaps his long experience in conquests, and the terrible bloodshed and cruelties he had witnessed, had created in Cabrillo an overwhelming desire to avoid violence. If that were true, he was unique among his contemporaries.

On Tuesday, October 3, they left San Diego Bay "and Wednesday, Thursday and Friday sailed on their course some eighteen leagues along the coast . . . At nightfall they were close to some islands which are about seven leagues from the mainland, and as the wind died out they could not reach them that night."

They had discovered the Channel Islands, which gird the southern California coast between San Diego and Santa Barbara. On Saturday at daybreak, when the wind freshened, they landed on Santa Catalina Island, directly opposite San Juan Capistrano, where 234 years later, in 1776, the mission famed for its swallows would be built. At that time California would still be the beautiful unspoiled land inhabited by Indians that it was on the day Cabrillo first gazed upon it.

As the ship's boat approached the beach on Santa Catalina, "a great number of Indians came out of the bushes and grass, shouting, dancing, and making signs not to come ashore. As from the boats they saw the women fleeing, they made signs to them not to fear; so shortly they [the men] became assured and put their bows and arrows on the ground." Here, once more, Cabrillo was told of other Spaniards inland.

They spent only a few hours on Santa Catalina, and then turned their ships back toward the coast. On Sunday, October 8, they entered another large bay which they named Los Fumos, "on account of the many smokes they saw there . . . it is an excellent harbor and the country is good, with many valleys, plains and groves of trees." This was San Pedro, now the great harbor of Los Angeles, and although many smokes may still be seen there, they come not from grass or Indian fires but from myriad industrial plants, oil wells, and freeways lacing the homeland of millions of persons. Indians in San Pedro also told them excitedly that other Spaniards were to be found toward the north.

The city of Los Angeles now stands where Cabrillo saw smoke rising as he entered the bay. He named the place Los Fumos.

The next port of call was only a short distance away. It is now known as Santa Monica Bay. The ships remained there overnight and then pointed again toward the northwest.

Now they passed through the beautiful Santa Barbara Channel, which lies between the lovely beaches of the California shore and the Channel Islands. This was the land inhabited by the Chumash Indians, and Cabrillo saw and visited many of their towns. He maintained constant vigilance for the mouth of a large river believed to exist in this area and to flow out of the land Coronado had reached. He asked all Indians with whom he talked if they knew of the river. They knew of several rivers farther north, and some they considered quite large. Cabrillo would go on, always with soaring hopes, but he would find neither a great river nor the Strait of Anian.

The culture of the Chumash Indians was superior to that of most southern California Indian tribes. Their houses were of grass or tule, dome-shaped and often fifty feet or more in diameter. As many as fifty persons lived in a single dwelling. The men were excellent canoe builders. Most Indians made canoes by digging out a single log, but the Chumash made them of planks lashed together and calked. Some of these seaworthy craft could carry as many as a score of persons. They made carved wooden dishes, sculptured figurines from stones, and painted figures on posts that were erected over graves and at places of worship. Most of the people were friendly.

". . . canoes kept coming out to the ships," says the summary, "and they pointed out that there were still larger canoes beyond. Tuesday, the 17th [October] they proceeded three leagues with favorable winds, and from daybreak many canoes went along with the ships, to whom the Captain always gave many presents. All this coast passed is very well settled, the Indians bringing them many very good fresh sardines. They say that inland there are many towns and much food, but they do not eat maize. They go dressed in skins and have very long hair tied up with some long cords. Inserted between the hair and these cords are many daggers made of flint, bone, and wood. The country appears to be excellent." Some Indians, however, resented the Spaniards' intrusion, and they would be an important factor in the outcome of the Cabrillo voyage.

Strong northwest winds forced the ships to turn out from the coast, and they made a landing on San Miguel Island, the northernmost of the chain, where they found a very good port inhabited by Chumash people. A storm arose, and they were held in the protected harbor for about a week.

Fall storms and adverse winds continued to beset them as they went on north, and on some days "they went beating about in one direction and another . . . without being able to gain any distance."

The month of November began with a howling northwest gale "which did not allow them to carry an inch of sail . . . they could do nothing but run back to shelter." Day after day, fighting cold, rain, heavy seas, and high winds, they pushed on, making landings when they could near Indian towns, and always inquiring for the "great river."

They found Monterey Bay but missed the Golden Gate. They saw the mountains of the coastal ranges, some of which had snow on them. The coast now appeared to be uninhabited, and was frighteningly bold, and the mountains "seem to reach the heavens, and the sea beats on them; sailing along close to land, it appears as if they would fall on the ships."

By mid-November they were near Point Arena, on the northern coast of California. For days and nights in the unceasing turbulence the men in the little *Victoria* "had passed through even greater hardships and perils than those on the *San Salvador* as she was small and had no covered deck . . . the sea was so high that it was frightful to see . . ."

Cabrillo, fearing that to continue would mean the loss of one or even both of the battered vessels and the lives of all the men, turned back. Running before the winds roaring out of the north Pacific, they reached safety once more on November 23 in the little harbor of San Miguel Island.

Here this passage appears in the voyage summary:

"While wintering . . . [at San Miguel Island] there passed from this present life, January 3, 1543, Juan Rodríguez Cabrillo, the captain of the ships, from a fall which he had in this island the previous time they were there, in which he broke an arm, close to the shoulder."

There is, however, evidence to show that the writer of the summary made mistakes in recounting the details of Cabrillo's death. Later testimony given by two men who had served with the expedition conformed generally in a quite different version of the tragedy.

Francisco de Vargas testified that with "the natives of this island he [Cabrillo] had some great fights as they came out in a warlike manner." During all the time the ships were at the island "the Indians never stopped fighting. One day, a large party of soldiers having gone ashore to take water, a number of Indians attacked them and handled them so roughly they were in danger. General Juan Rodríguez [Cabrillo], seeing from the ship the difficulties in which the Indians had his men and hearing the clamor, hurried up to give them assistance. He himself with some soldiers went ashore, and as they were landing his foot slipped from the boat and his shinbone was shattered on a rock. From this he died on his own ship in ten or twelve days, first having extracted his soldiers from the dangers in which they were."

Lazaro de Cárdenas declared that as Cabrillo, after returning to San Miguel, "was going ashore in a boat with some soldiers he fell between some rocks and broke a leg. From this

Cabrillo suffered a fatal injury when he fell on the rocks on San Miguel Island.

fall a fatal illness ensued from which he died within twelve days and was buried there. Before the end he called Captain Ferrer and gave him the appointment as captain-general . . ."

The grave of Cabrillo has never been found.

In his dying hours he had "admonished and begged" Ferrer to continue the exploration of the northwest coast, for he and several others who were there believed they were not far from the Orient.

Ferrer made a brave attempt to comply with Cabrillo's last wishes. When the ships were reconditioned, Ferrer set out from San Miguel Island late in January 1543. Fighting violent weather almost constantly, the vessels became separated far at sea off the coast. However, they had sailed north of the point reached by Cabrillo, perhaps in the latitude of the present California-Oregon border, before Ferrer gave up the fight.

Not until the 26th of March, when they were far down the coast of Baja California at the Isla de Cedros, were the vessels reunited. They were "delighted and gave many thanks to the Lord."

On Saturday, April 14, they sailed into the little harbor of Navidad, which they had left nearly ten months earlier.

4

The Way Home

THE IMMENSE REGION THAT
would become American California had been touched from
two sides—from the deserts bordering the Colorado River and
from the Pacific Ocean.

Yet the feats of Alarcón, Díaz and Cabrillo were held to be
of little importance by the Spanish government. The frontiers
of New Spain had been extended great distances to the north,
but that was all that had been accomplished. No treasure had
been discovered. Certainly the areas Alarcón and Díaz had
reached were worthless, and the northwest coast seen by Cabrillo presented nothing more than a forbidding barrier abut-
ting raging seas. No evidence had been obtained to indicate
that precious metals were to be found behind its frowning
face.

The Indians were poor, naked, fish-eating savages, and possessed nothing of value to trade. It would, of course, be gratify-
ing if they could be converted to the Christian faith, and some
day that must be accomplished. At the moment, though, con-
version was not enough reward to justify the expenditures of
the money and manpower necessary to establish a mission

colony on the remote northwest coast. Moreover, similar religious undertakings much closer to Mexico were straining the resources of both the Church and the treasury of New Spain.

Before the sixteenth century had ended, however, events would take place that once more would focus the attention of the Spanish King and the Viceroy on the northern California coast.

The history of California now turns far across the Pacific to the Philippines. Ferdinand Magellan, sailing from Spain through the strait at the southern tip of South America that now bears his name and across the Pacific, had reached these islands in 1521. He had been killed by natives, but one of his ships completed the first circumnavigation of the world.

Between 1527 and 1564 several Spanish vessels had made the Pacific crossing from the west coast of Mexico. The prevailing easterly trade winds made the voyage relatively easy, but returning such a great distance against those winds was virtually impossible. Several attempts had failed, and the discovery of a return route to Mexico became the major objective of explorers sailing under the Spanish flag.

There was a very good reason why Spain was eager to discover a feasible route eastward across the Pacific from the Philippines—a fabulously lucrative trade. To the Philippines from China went large junks laden with raw silk, embroidered velvet, brocades of gold and silver upon silk, gilt and white porcelain, pearls, rubies, sapphires, crystal, fine furniture handcarved from rare tropical woods, linens, nutmeg, cinnamon, licorice, ginger, inlaid chests, china, gold and brass pieces, and countless knickknacks. For New Spain silver, these valuable products could be obtained at extremely low prices.

The Viceroy, now Luis de Velasco, had appointed Miguel López de Legaspi to command an expedition to the Philippines with three specific purposes in mind: (1) subdue and take full possession of the islands, (2) establish a settlement to serve as a base for the trade with China, and (3) discover a return route for galleons to New Spain.

Legaspi was a man of excellent reputation. More than fifty years of age, he had lived in Mexico for twenty-two years and had performed notably in the royal service. With five vessels carrying more than three hundred men he sailed from Navidad late in November 1564.

Accompanying him was a contingent of five friars led by Andrés de Urdaneta, an Augustinian of remarkable attainments. A highly skilled navigator, he had been with Alvarado in Guatemala, had been captain of a flotilla sent to Peru, and had made other voyages. In his early life he had served as a military officer. He had taken his vows as a friar in 1552. On the trip with Legaspi, in addition to his religious duties, he would serve in an advisory capacity to the pilots and captains.

The faith the Spanish government, from King Philip II down to the colonial officials, held in the abilities of Urdaneta was reflected in the instructions given Legaspi. In part these said: "As you are aware that Fray Andrés de Urdaneta is going on this voyage by the orders of His Majesty, you will see to it that he comes back in one of the ships you send for the discovery of the return route . . . confidence is felt that he will be the principal factor in finding the return route to New Spain on account of his experience, the knowledge he has of the weather in those parts, and his other qualities."

Thus the stage was set and the orders were given for Urdaneta to make the great discovery that would bring untold riches to the treasury of Spain. But, as the poet Robert Burns would write some two centuries later:

> The best laid schemes o' mice and men
> Gang aft a-gley . . .

A few days after leaving Navidad, one of Legaspi's ships deserted and vanished into the west. It was the little *San Lucas*, of only forty tons burden, and actually designated to serve as a tender or dispatch boat for the fleet. Its commander was Don Alonso de Arellano, its pilot was Lope Martín, a capable navigator, and it carried a crew of twenty men.

Arellano was a member of one of the noblest families of Spain, and a relative of Cortez, the conqueror of Mexico. Of Lope Martín's background almost nothing is known, but he appears to have been a bold adventurer of unsavory character. He would serve some time in jail. Later he would be marooned on the Isla de Barbudos following a mutiny, in which the captain of the ship on which he was then serving was murdered.

The *San Lucas*, a fast sailer, reached the Philippines early in 1565, well ahead of the flotilla. Arellano made no effort to rejoin Legaspi. He had only one objective—to beat Urdaneta back to New Spain, winning for himself the credit and a financial reward for discovering the return route.

Legaspi took possession of the Philippines for Spain, founded a permanent settlement, and established a base for a rich trade that would continue for three centuries. These activities consumed several months, and it was not until June 1 that he complied with his order to dispatch Urdaneta in search of a feasible return route. By that time Arellano had been on the way more than a month.

Arellano and Martín were aware, as were Urdaneta and the other navigators with Legaspi, that the prevailing winds on the northwest coast of California came from the west and north. That knowledge had been gained by Cabrillo and other voyagers. Therefore, when Arellano left the Phillippines, on April 22, 1565, he sailed on courses to the north and northeast. He later claimed to have observed wondrous sights as the

strong winds took him on a zigzagging route across the unknown north Pacific. Among them were pelicans larger than
ostriches, black birds with frightful screams, barking sea-dogs
with feet and hands and sharply pointed ears, and porpoises as
big as cows. The men on the *San Lucas* suffered greatly from
malnutrition, thirst, and bitter cold. At one time they encountered a blizzard, and the temperature fell so low that some oil
in a demijohn was frozen hard.

Running before strong north winds for a number of days in
June, Arellano apparently did not see the coast of American
California. It is believed that his first sight of land came at
daylight on July 17 near Punta Abreojos, midway down the
peninsula of Baja California. During the final days of the voyage they encountered fierce storms. The sailors were so weak
from scurvy that they had difficulty handling the sails, but on
August 9 they reached the harbor of Navidad.

In a tiny vessel, without adequate supplies and equipment,
Arellano had completed one of the most daring feats in all the
long history of maritime exploration. He had proved that a
great-circle course to the north was a feasible return route for
galleons carrying cargoes from the Philippines to New Spain.
But he received neither honor nor reward for his invaluable
discovery.

In the *San Pablo*, a stout, well-equipped, and adequately
manned vessel of three hundred tons, more than seven times
larger than the *San Lucas*, Urdaneta followed much of Arellano's course. He struck the coast, however, considerably farther north, in the vicinity of San Miguel Island, where Cabrillo
had been mortally injured.

Two pilots accompanying Urdaneta kept logs of the voyage,
but he apparently wrote very little about it. As far as is known
he recounted only that they had reached Acapulco early in
October 1565, and "what with contrary winds and sickness,

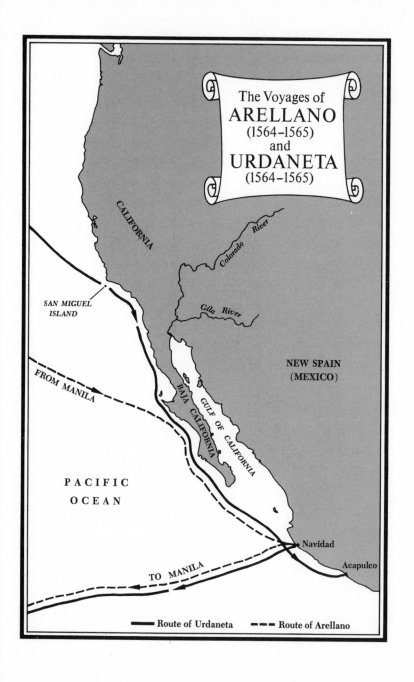

The Voyages of
ARELLANO
(1564–1565)
and
URDANETA
(1564–1565)

CALIFORNIA

Colorado River

Gila River

SAN MIGUEL
ISLAND

FROM MANILA

NEW SPAIN
(MEXICO)

BAJA CALIFORNIA

GULF OF CALIFORNIA

PACIFIC
OCEAN

TO MANILA

Navidad

Acapulco

Route of Urdaneta   Route of Arellano

we passed through great hardships. Sixteen died before entering in the port, and four others afterwards, besides an Indian
of the Ladrones whom the General [Legaspi] sent, and three
other Indians from Zubu [Cebu]. Felipe de Salcedo, the
grandson of the General, came as captain of the ship and carried himself very well in the discharge of his duty."

It was, after all, Urdaneta who was hailed as the discoverer
of the return route. He was a friend of the King, the Viceroy,
and many other high personages in both the royal court and
the government of New Spain. Moreover, he was an Augustinian friar, and the historians of that religious order were un-
stinting in their praise of him. They conveniently forgot about
the matchless feat of Arellano.

The Spanish government attempted to keep the discovery of
the return route from the Philippines an official secret, but the
news was soon widespread. The result was that within a few
years British buccaneers were striking along the western coast
of New Spain and capturing Spanish ships. The raids made it
obvious that a naval base must be established, preferably at
some place along the northwest coast Cabrillo had reached, so
that galleons returning from the Orient could be protected
and convoyed by warships to Acapulco. A good port on the
northern coast would also make it possible for galleons to take
on wood and fresh water and restore the health of their crews
after the long ordeal of crossing the Pacific.

Now, once again, the eyes and thoughts of New Spain officials were focused on American California. This time, however, they were concentrating their attention more on safeguarding treasure than finding it.

Until the year 1578 no enemy had disrupted the smooth
flow of Spanish commerce on the western coasts of either
North or South America. Treasure ships unloaded at Panama,

Acapulco, and other Pacific ports. They brought not only precious metals from New World mines for transshipment overland to Atlantic harbors, but valuable cargoes from the Philippines. Spain considered this immense part of the Pacific, more popularly known as the Southern Sea, her own private domain and thought it safe from all intruders. Then suddenly into it swept the red-bearded English privateer, Francis Drake, in the *Golden Hind*.

If he had appeared without warning out of the sky, the Spanish would have been no more surprised. He struck with the fury and devastating effect of a tropical tempest. Within a short time his cargo hold was virtually bulging with gold, silver, pearls, and "goodly greate emeralds" as long as a man's finger. From one Spanish galleon alone he took "greate riches, as jewels and precious stones, thirteen chests full of real of plate, fourscore pound weight of gold, and six and twenty tons of silver." From another Spanish vessel he obtained "a store of fruits, conserves and sugars, a quantity of jewels and precious stones, 13 chests of plate, 8 pound weight of gold, 26 tuns of uncoined silver, two large silver and gilt bowls, valued in all to 360 thousand pezoes, which was the cause of her slow sailing." Drake did not destroy this ship after looting it. He amused himself by giving its captain in exchange for all this treasure "a little linen . . . and so dismissed him to go on his voyage with more speed" in an empty vessel.

Drake had reached the Pacific through the Strait of Magellan, but he did not propose to return through "its hell darke nights and the mercyless fury of tempestuous storms." As Spanish warships sought to intercept him, he disappeared to the north.

Now the Spanish were not only horrified by what had happened, but were completely confused and filled with growing apprehension. Their fear sprang not only from the realization

Francis Drake intercepts a galleon loaded with treasure.

that if one Englishman could invade their South Sea others certainly could follow, but also from the suspicion that Drake had discovered the long-sought Northwest Passage, the Strait of Anian. If this were not true, some argued, why would he sail to the north? There was no treasure to be found on the northern California coast. But another contention appeared to be more logical. It was that Drake was hoping to waylay a loaded galleon coming from the Orient.

The truth was that Drake was looking for the Northwest Passage. The observations he took as he pushed northward along the California coast, however, told him that the continent grew steadily wider toward the north, and the Atlantic, which was so close to the Pacific at Panama, was thousands of miles east of him and was becoming more distant with the passage of every league. His chaplain, the Reverend Francis Fletcher, an untiring and prolific chronicler, recorded that they ran into violent winds, "vile, thicke, and stinking fogges . . . extreame and nipping cold . . ." The ropes of the ship were frozen stiff, and they were forced to turn back south. Fletcher reported their latitude at the time as being 48 degrees north, which, if correct, would have placed them off the Olympic Peninsula of the present State of Washington, almost to Puget Sound.

The *Golden Hind* was badly in need of repairs, and in the middle of June 1579, Drake put into "a convenient and fit harborough." There he remained about a month, calking and scraping the ship, he and his men enjoying a much needed respite from the ordeals of the sea. The exact site of this landing has never been indisputably determined. Some authorities believe it was made in Bodega Bay, just north of Point Reyes, but others think it was closer to the entrance of the Golden Gate, in the bay that now bears Drake's name.

Crowds of Indians made peaceful visits to Drake's camp,

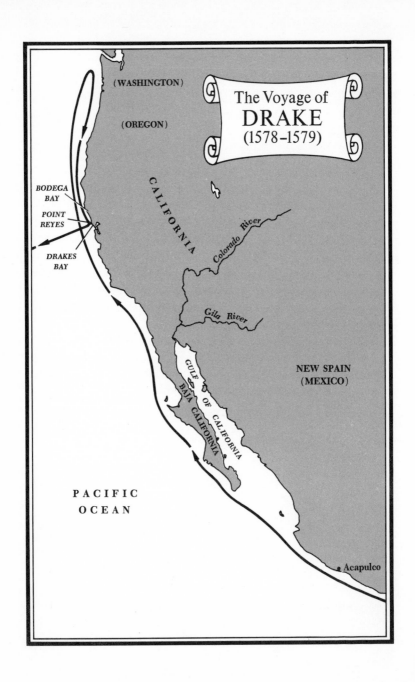

and from their gestures Fletcher concluded that they were imploring Drake "to take the Province and kingdom into his hand, and become their king and patron; making signs that they would resigne unto him their right and title in the whole land, and become his vassals in themselves and their posterities . . ."

These people probably were Pomos, who inhabited the present Russian River Valley. Fletcher believed he heard them use the word *Amen*, but as he was a preacher that may have been more a wish than a reality. In the first account of them to be written, he described them as "people of a tractable, free and loving nature, without guile or treachery . . . so strong of body, that which 2 or 3 of our men could hardly beare, one of them would take upon his back, and without grudging carry it easily away . . ."

Drake took possession of California for Queen Elizabeth, erected a monument, "namely a plate of brasse, fast nailed to a great and firme post; whereon is engraven her graces name, and the day and year of our arrival . . ." Then he sailed away across the Pacific and went home by way of the Cape of Good Hope and the Atlantic.

The officials of New Spain had no knowledge of Drake's whereabouts, and continued to keep watch for him. When, after the passage of two years, he had failed to reappear, they began to breathe easier. Galleons continued to come from the Philippines, but although Drake was gone and no other British pirates had appeared, losses of ships continued. The weather and the seas were greater enemies on the long voyage than buccaneers.

Yet some officials advanced arguments against establishing a relief haven on the northwest coast, declaring that maintaining it and a garrison at such a great distance from Acapulco

would be both difficult and costly. Most captains, they as-
serted, preferred to stay well off shore, rather than take the
risk of entering an unknown haven, even though a respite
from the ordeals of the crossing would have been welcome. It
was very difficult to take the big cumbersome galleons into a
small port. Only an excellent harbor with an entrance protected from winds and adverse currents would serve the
purpose.

The opponents of the proposal chose to ignore the fact, if
they knew of it, that Cabrillo had discovered a port at San
Diego suitable for the purpose in every respect. Perhaps Cabrillo's narrative had been forgotten, for even those urging
that the station be established failed to refer to it. It is possible, as well, that the supporters thought that building a base
farther north than San Diego would be more practical, since
ships from the Orient would reach it in less time. If this were
true, it was a mistake, for most ships returning from Manila
first sighted the coast not a great distance from San Diego,
either north or south of it.

In February 1584, the *Santa María de Jesús* reached Acapulco after a seven months' voyage from Manila. The masts of
the ship had been broken, and scarcely enough rigging remained to sail it. On the trip the captain, master, pilot, and
fifty-six sailors and passengers had died of scurvy. Deeply
stirred by this tragedy and the losses of other vessels returning
from the Orient, Father Pedro Moya y Contreras, who was
politically influential and prominent in Philippine affairs,
wrote the Spanish King:

> When the ships come from China, they sight the coast of
> New Spain 700 leagues before reaching Acapulco, and from
> there sail almost in sight of land. Although it may be neces-
> sary to land to repair the ships, or to take on a supply of

water or other things, they cannot do so as the ports on all that coast are not known, nor have they any place in which to take shelter from the contrary winds which ordinarily blow in that quarter. The same thing happens to ships which before reaching the coast encounter storms . . . they have to return to the islands from which they sailed, as there is no port on the coast.

Even Father Moya did not mention Cabrillo's San Diego, undoubtedly for reasons best known to himself, but he did bring up some other interesting matters. He continued:

In order that all this may come to an end, and Your Majesty may have knowledge of all that coast which some say runs to join the mainland of China, and others that it terminates in a strait called "Anian" which continues to and ends nears Ireland, I have ordered two *fragatas* [small ships] built to search for and discover all the ports, islands, rivers, mountains and settlements which there are or may be on all that coast, by what people of what languages it is inhabited and settled, what is their dress and mode of living, and what fruits and other useful things they have, taking the latitude of everything and finding out everything . . . As this business seems so important, I beg Your Majesty not to be displeased that it has been done without consulting you . . . it will not all told cost I believe more than eight or ten thousand pesos. Besides what has been said, this voyage may have another result, namely that by this way and at less cost than by land it will be possible to communicate with and serve New Mexico while being settled, as . . . it is understood to be very near the coast. All together, it is calculated to save souls with greater facility, which is the principal object of Your Majesty.

Father Moya's correspondence suggests that he was thinking as much about converting the savages of California as about new discoveries, but he fully understood the trend of official thinking, which was toward safeguarding the Manila galleons. He stressed that objective, aware that wherever conquests and explorations were undertaken, missionaries inevitably played dominant roles in them. If a northern California base were established, the Church would be well represented.

The Council of the Indies mildly rebuked Moya for ordering the building of two *fragatas* at government expense without official authorization and without previously advising His Majesty of his intentions. The King himself, however, did not seem to be greatly annoyed. Viceroy Velasco had died and had been succeeded by the Marqués de Villamanrique, and the King wrote him for more information about Moya's schemes.

Villamanrique was not in sympathy with the projected policies of either his predecessor, Velasco, or Moya. He was opposed to spending money on more voyages of discovery on the northwest coast and to establishing a base north of Baja California.

"The coast of [New] Spain," he wrote the sovereign, "is known on the side of the South Sea as high as 42° 54', as ships coming from the Philippines have made land in that latitude* . . . Along all this coast it has not seemed advisable to make any settlement, for the reason that no ship has been in danger there because of the absence of one.† According to the relations given to you . . . most of the people on that coast are savage and poor, maintaining themselves by fishing. As making a settlement there now would bring some inconvenience, and none appears from not having made one, it will be well not to treat about it if Your Majesty would now be served . . . Respecting the idea [advanced by Moya] of

---

* Approximately at Cape Blanco, Oregon. This was a statement without foundation.
† Also an untruth.

communicating from that sea and coast with the discoveries in New Mexico, it appears, according to the map, that this is a country between the seas, and up to the present it is not known whether it be nearest the North Sea [Atlantic] or so near the South Sea that this can be done from there, as Your Majesty has been informed."

Either Villamanrique was ignorant of existing information or he was being deceptive, for it was well understood in Mexico City that New Mexico was much closer to the Colorado River and the Gulf of California, as well as to the Pacific, than to the Atlantic. Villamanrique, however, stubbornly adhered to his opinions, although events had occurred that provided him with good reasons to change his mind.

5

The Search for a Port

LATE IN 1584 INTO ACAPULCO from the Orient sailed Francisco Gali in the *San Juan Bautista*. Gali had been in the service of the King all his life, and was a distinguished pilot and a noted cosmographer. He reported that he was convinced he had come close to discovering the Pacific mouth of the long-sought Strait of Anian.

After sailing east by north, said Gali, "and having covered 300 leagues eastward from Japan, I came across a heavy swell, which came from north and northwest, an extensive open ocean, which however did not stop our progress and which did not become calm or go down, whatever wind was blowing; and I found the same to be the case always until I had sailed more than 700 leagues. When I found myself at a distance of 200 leagues from the coast of New Spain, this sea ceased, which seemed to me to be a sign that it was the strait that goes between the mainland of New Spain and Asia and Tartary. During these 700 leagues I saw a great number of whales, tunny, mackerel, and bonitos, fishes which usually haunt straits and currents, where they spawn; from which I concluded that it was a strait."

Gali sighted the California coast just south of San Francisco Bay, and at "a distance of 4 leagues from land I found great bunches of roots and leaves and canes and a number of seals, which made me believe there must be many rivers and good harbours on the whole of this coast . . ."

Time would tell, of course, that Gali had not been near a great strait through which sailing ships could pass, that none existed. On his circle course he had sailed across one of the richest fishing grounds in the world, the North Pacific. But he was very correct about one thing: there were many rivers pouring their immense floods into the sea, the rivers of Oregon and northern California rushing down from towering snow-capped ranges, mountains too far inland to be visible to him, mountains no man but Indians had ever seen.

The Spanish government now took the position that it would be advantageous to have ships homing from the Orient look for a relief port as they sailed southward along the coast.

Gali, with a long record of reliability, was sent back in the *San Juan Bautista* to the Philippines, with orders to sail from there to explore the California coast as far as possible to the north. By the time he reached Manila, however, the *San Juan Bautista* was in such bad condition that it was deemed unfit for such a dangerous voyage. Before another vessel could be built for him, Gali died.

Pedro de Unamuno, who had been Gali's second in command, was named to succeed him and to undertake the exploration. Of Unamuno nothing is known, except that he was recognized as a highly capable navigator and was respected by some high Spanish officials.

Before he could sail from Manila, Unamuno got into trouble. Two ships had been assigned to him, the larger of which was armed, and a totally unfounded rumor was spread

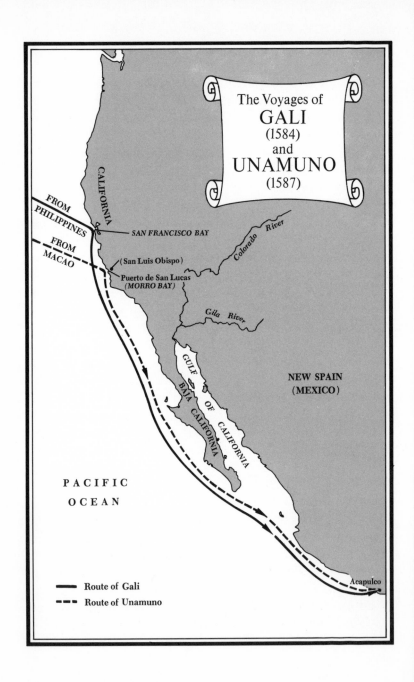

that he intended to become a pirate. Also a report was
circulated that he was in league with some Portuguese merchants in Macao and planned to go there for the purpose of
carrying out a secret trade agreement with them. Since the
Portuguese had closed the port of Macao to Spanish vessels,
such an act would have violated both Spanish and Portuguese
regulations, and a court investigation was ordered. The hearings, which resulted in a judicial ruling forbidding Unamuno
to go to Macao, delayed him from leaving Manila until the
fall of 1586.

Unamuno had no intention of becoming a buccaneer, and
no evidence was produced to indicate that he harbored such a
scheme, but he did ignore the court order, went straight to
Macao, and proceeded to take on Portuguese cargo for
Mexico. A disloyal person with him informed Portuguese authorities of his disobedience. His ships were seized, and he and
his officers were put in jail and ordered to stand trial. Unamuno's defense was that bad weather and a lack of supplies
had forced him to put into Macao. He won his freedom, but
his troubles were not ended.

The Spanish had got word of his illegal action and sent officers from the Philippines to take the ships from him. Both
vessels, loaded with merchandise, were returned to Manila.
Now he was "on the beach" in Macao, without a ship.

Unamuno was a courageous and resourceful man, however,
and he soon managed to purchase a small vessel. Just how this
transaction was accomplished is not known, but there are reasons to believe that the necessary funds came from two
sources, Macao merchants and a high-ranking Franciscan
priest, Fray Martín Ignacio de Loyola, a nephew of the great
founder of the Jesuits, Ignacio de Loyola. Father Martín was
in Macao after becoming involved in a bitter conflict between
religious orders in China. He had been badly treated, and was

eager to return to Spain and make a report about the situation in the Orient to the King.

Unamuno's ship was a *fragata*, a small single-decked, three-masted craft, probably of no more than forty tons burden. Only men of incomparable daring would have set out in such a frail vessel to cross the tempestuous North Pacific. Father Martín would say nothing more than that the undertaking "seemed like temerity, but I never took my life into account in serving God and the King." How Unamuno and others felt is not revealed in the sparse reports of the voyage that have survived. One thing is known: Unamuno was determined to carry out the orders given to Gali to explore the northwest coast.

The name of the *fragata* has been lost to history. On board, besides Unamuno and Father Martín, were a pilot, Alonso Gómez, two other Franciscan priests, a young Japanese, only a few sailors, because experienced crewmen were not easily obtained for a Spanish vessel in Macao, and a number of Spanish soldiers and Luzon Indians, who had accompanied Unamuno from Manila—perhaps forty men in all.

Loaded with Portuguese trade goods, the *fragata* cleared Macao on Sunday, July 12, 1587.

For more than three months the sturdy little ship and the strong men fought the raging seas, fogs, and cold winds of the North Pacific. An indication of the ordeals they faced is found in Unamuno's log entry of August 31: ". . . our mainmast broke in two, as well as the foremast and bowsprit. After we had repaired them as best we could, in order to be able to navigate, we continued . . . and went up to latitude 39 degrees." Four days later, on September 3, "an east-northeast wind struck us, so we could go no farther north . . . the masts were sprung, the vessel was small, and those aboard had little protection, not having come as well prepared to resist the cold and wet as was advisable."

On October 17, a lookout thought that he saw land, but "as it was not clear, the land being covered with a thick mist, we were not certain . . . That night, during the first watch . . . we came upon two very small islands . . . We came so close to them (within an harquebus-shot) that had we not been keeping a good watch on account of the fog, we would have been lost. We stood out to sea until the morning watch."

They had reached the California coast in the vicinity of Morro Bay. Passing through great beds of kelp, they came into protected quiet waters and anchored off a long sandy beach. Before them were high rolling hills and valley lands covered with live oaks, and tree-clad mountains stood farther eastward against a blue sky. It was October 18, the day of San Lucas, "and we therefore named it [Morro Bay] Puerto de San Lucas."

Two Indians were seen on shore, but they made no signal to the ship, and "a council was held of those on board and, all being assembled, it was considered what should be done, and whether some soldiers should land and explore the neighborhood of the harbor . . . since it was for this purpose that we came. All were agreed that the Captain and twelve soldiers and some [Luzon] natives, armed with swords and shields, should land and make a reconnaissance of the vicinity . . . I landed with twelve soldiers with their coats of mail and harquebuses, Fr. Martín Ignacio in advance carrying a cross in his hands, and with some Luzon natives with their swords and shields."

This is the first known *entrada* of the California mainland from the sea. It resulted in fighting with Indians in which men on both sides were killed and wounded.

In the course of three days Unamuno and his party marched inland to the vicinity of the present city of San Luis Obispo, passing along pleasant streams that meandered through a

lovely land of great hills patched with groves of oaks and syca-
mores. Unamuno thought the harbor in which the *fragata* was
anchored ideal for a base for homeward-bound ships from the
Orient, for there was "an unlimited quantity of fish of different kinds, trees suitable for masts, [fresh] water, firewood,
and abundant shellfish with all of which a ship in need could
supply itself."

Unamuno admonished his men to watch diligently for signs
of gold and silver. It was his hope that they would encounter
friendly Indians, of whom he could inquire whether any precious metals or jewels were to be found in the country. The
first excursion inland took place on Sunday, October 18. Numerous Indian trails were found, and after a consultation "it
was agreed to follow one of them, which led southeast toward
a high hill from whence what lay about could be seen. With
Father Martín leading, his cross in his hand, we set off towards it, two of our Luzon natives ahead as scouts." The
scouts soon reported having seen five Indians some distance
ahead, and "we hastened our pace in order to speak with them
. . . The sergeant went ahead with the scouts after the five
persons, and although he made every effort they could not be
overtaken . . . They were naked and fleet . . ."

Four men were detached to climb a hill, "and from there to
look about to see if there were any settlements or other indications of people, and to find out if there were any minerals in
the hill." Neither Indians nor anything of value was discovered, but Unamuno thought the hill "a suitable place to take
possession in His Majesty's name of the port and the country." When the ceremonies were concluded they returned to
the ship.

Before dawn the next morning, October 19, Unamuno
again set out to explore. With him this time were another
priest, Father Noguera, twelve Spaniards, and eight Luzon na-

After exploring the countryside, Unamuno climbed a hill to claim the land for the King of Spain.

tives, all well armed. They ". . . followed the trail leading eastward which the day previous had seemed the most beaten. Advancing as noiselessly as possible, when day dawned we had journeyed two leagues without having seen or heard anything of settlement, smoke or person. We then drew aside towards the slope of a hill under some oaks . . . and lying there in ambush, we watched all that valley as far as we could see until an hour after sunrise. We could not see any settlement or any people . . .

"From here we set out up river towards the east [probably the present Chorro Valley and the creek of the same name] . . . and found many footprints . . . After marching about two leagues . . . we came upon an old Indian camp . . . From these huts we marched half a league up the river . . . Here the men ate and rested and on account of the great heat we remained here until about three o'clock in the afternoon."

Unamuno then led his little company on "toward a great gap which showed to the east." Reaching the foot of a high hill near the gap, he sent six men to climb to the top of it and "from there to look in every direction to see if they could see any settlement, people or fires, and also to ascertain whether there were any minerals in it."

Upon returning the scouts reported they could see nothing from the hilltop but empty country. As they had brought with them only enough supplies for one night, they turned back, "realizing that it would not be wise to march farther into unknown territory with so few men . . ." They camped "an hour before nightfall under three great black oak trees . . . and rested there that night with sentries posted . . ."

While Unamuno had been exploring inland on October 19, trouble had occurred on the shore off which the ship was anchored. Father Martín had led a group toward the southwest of the port, where they had seen smoke. One Spaniard, Vallejeda, and several Luzon natives remained at the creek to "fetch water and firewood." Suddenly twenty-three Indians appeared out of a pine forest, and two of them "came to the river to talk with Vallejeda, who carried only his sword."

Angry shouts and gestures convinced Vallejeda "that matters were coming to a bad pass." He attempted to pacify the Indians with several gifts, but more came down the hill and took from the Luzon natives "some clothes and the casks they had brought for the water . . . At this juncture, Father Martín and the others, who had gone to see what there was in the southwest, were seen approaching." Quickly the Indians tried to force Vallejeda and the wood-gatherers to leave with them, but they saved themselves by leaping into the water. Men on the ship opened fire with their harquebuses and the Indians retreated up the hill.

Shortly afterward the Indians "separated into three parties and attacked our men, showing every evidence of a wish to kill them, and shot many arrows at them, but without doing any damage. Father Martín would not allow any harquebuses to be fired until it appeared that they were getting arrogant, and then they fired at the Indians and wounded some, compelling them to draw back to the top of the hill." The shore party got safely back aboard the ship as dusk was falling.

Unamuno had no name for the Indians, but they undoubtedly were Salinans, a small linguistic stock inhabiting the area of San Luis Obispo and Monterey counties at the time. They dwelt in houses of brush or grass and had no canoes. They hunted more than they fished, but depended for their subsistence principally on vegetable food, such as acorns and grass seed. They used stone mortars and coiled baskets. Little else is known to science about them. Like most California tribes, they decreased in number rapidly after the building of the Spanish missions, and were virtually extinct by 1900.

Returning on October 20 from their exploration, Unamuno and his men were within sight of the ship and could see the ship's boat waiting for them when they were attacked, and "Aranguren and Mendoza came up with many arrow and javelin wounds, and immediately after them, Ynfanzon with many arrow wounds. They would have been killed except for timely support. As Contreras had taken off his coat of mail, he was wounded by a javelin which passed entirely through his breast, so that he could not retreat . . . he died immediately. With him they killed one of our Luzon natives with a javelin which he failed to ward off with his shield."

Fire from the guns of the Spaniards drove the Indians back, but they soon charged again, and "an order was given to look to the wounded and for the rest to close ranks. In view of the great number of Indians, we endeavored to reach the beach in our order, as that was the best point from which to defend ourselves."

They were now joined by the men who had come ashore in the ship's boat, and "we had a fight and skirmish with the Indians in which some of them were killed and many wounded, only one of our men being wounded." Once more the Indians retreated, and Unamuno ordered a raft built, as "in this we might all embark together, the ship's boat being too small to take us on board except in many trips . . ." While the raft was being constructed "the enemy attacked us on three fronts but withdrew with loss without wounding any of our men. It was about five in the afternoon when the enemy retired . . . we embarked on the raft and the ship's boat."

After supper on the little *fragata* a council was held "to consider whether the next day we should land to fight the enemy, or continue on our voyage." Much of their powder supply had been accidentally destroyed, and "it was resolved that it was better to continue our voyage, coasting along the land, and not go ashore after the Indians . . . our men were badly wounded and medicine with which to treat them was scanty, and the unwounded men were too few to resist the enemy without powder or munitions; further, we had done in that port what was necessary to be done, and we could search for other harbors along the coast. It was therefore thought better to go and report to His Excellency [the Viceroy] on what had occurred . . ."

On October 21, before daybreak, the *fragata* left Morro Bay, sailing southward with difficulty against contrary winds. On the 23rd, in the afternoon, "a west-northwest wind blew up with such thick weather that we could not see the land for five days, although we were always within two leagues of it, and even less."

When on October 29 they "came into much disturbed white water, which seemed to be river water," they made an effort to move in close enough to determine if there was a harbor in the vicinity, but were turned back by fog and dangerous reefs. "As we could not land in the ship's boat, on account of its small size and the somewhat heavy sea running, and as the weather did not clear up . . . and because the wounded men were badly off for lack of medicine," Unamuno decided to abandon the effort to explore more of the coast.

On November 22, 1587, one hundred and thirty-four days after leaving Macao, Unamuno brought the *fragata* into the harbor of Acapulco.

Although Unamuno had accomplished a courageous feat, he was soon forgotten. Morro Bay did not appear on charts given to later explorers. No reference was made to his voyage in official papers after the Spanish government was notified that it had been completed and Father Martín had complained to both the King and the Viceroy of New Spain of the treatment Unamuno received in the Philippines and Macao.

Ships continued to arrive from the Philippines badly damaged and in danger of foundering. Many crewmen died of scurvy and the ordeals of the long voyage. Moreover, only a few days before Unamuno reached Acapulco another British raider struck along the Pacific coast of New Spain with devastating effect. The need for a haven on the northwest coast and of having warships escort the galleons to safety was forcefully demonstrated. But Villamanrique would do little or nothing to relieve the desperate situation.

Thomas Cavendish, scion of an old English family, inherited a fortune as a young man. By 1586 he had spent most of it in extravagant living and in financing sea adventures, one of which was a trip in his own ship to Virginia. With the money he had left and the credit available to him, he then equipped and armed three vessels, the *Desire*, the *Content*, and the *Gallant*, and became a buccaneer.

His flotilla sailed from Plymouth, England, in the summer of 1586, crossed the Atlantic, passed through the Strait of Magellan, and by the beginning of 1587 was moving northward along the coast of Chile intent upon capturing Spanish vessels.

Through the summer and fall of 1587, Cavendish took several prizes on the high seas and raided a number of Spanish ports as he continued to move northward until he had reached central Mexico. Brutal and barbaric, he tortured and hanged captured sailors, and wantonly burned churches, homes, and anchored ships. In one place he encountered stiff resistance from Spaniards and was driven off after losing a number of his men. This reversal left him with insufficient sailors for three ships. He sank the *Gallant* and went on with the *Content* and the *Desire*.

He would boast in a letter to one of his British patrons: "I navigated along the coast of Chile, Peru and New Spain, where I made great spoiles: I burnt and sunke 19 sailes of ships small and great. All the villages and townes that ever I landed at, I burnt and spoiled . . ."

From a Frenchman who was serving on a Spanish ship he had captured, Cavendish learned that a galleon was soon due to arrive from the Philippines. After repairing his vessels and taking on wood and water in Mazatlán Bay, he set out to lie in wait for it near Cape San Lucas, at the tip of the Baja California peninsula.

The galleon, the *Santa Ana*, a big-bellied vessel of six hundred tons burden, came in sight on November 4. It carried no cannon. Both the *Content* and the *Desire* mounted heavy guns. Against these great odds the Spaniards fought courageously to escape.

Between seven and eight o'clock in the morning, wrote Francis Pretty, master of the *Desire*, "the trumpeter of the ship going up into the top espied a sayle bearing from the sea with the cape, where upon hee cried out with no small joy to himselfe and the whole company, A sayle, a sayle, with which cheerfull word the master of the ship and divers others of the company went also up into the maine top, perceiving the speech to be very true gave information unto our Generall of these happy news, who was no lesse glad than the cause required; whereupon he gave in charge presently unto the whole company to put all things in readiness . . ."

The exciting pursuit of the great prize lasted for four hours. As the afternoon began, the English ships got close enough to the *Santa Ana* to fire, and gave the victim "the broad side of our great ordinance and a volee of small shot, and presently layed the ship aboard, whereof the king of Spaine was owner, which was Admiral of the South Sea, called the S. Anna & thought to be 700 tunnes in burthen."

The men of the *Santa Ana* had erected wooden screens to protect themselves from small-arms fire, and had "layed their sails close on their poope, their midship, with their fore castle, and having not one man to be seene, stood close under fights [barricades], with lances, javelins, rapiers . . . and an inumerable sort of great stones . . ."

The Spaniards, armed only with these ineffective weapons, nevertheless were able to repel boarding parties from Cavendish's ships. They threw stones, recounted Pretty, "upon our heads and into our ship so fast and being so many of them, they put us off againe, with the loss of 2 of our men which were slaine, and with the hurting of 4 or 5."

Now the attackers "trimmed our sailes, and fitted every man his furniture [weapons], and gave them a fresh encounter with our great ordinance, and also with our small shot, raking them through and through, to the killing and maiming of many of their men. Their Captaine still like a valiant man with his company stood very stoutly . . . not yielding as yet."

Driven off again by the determined Spaniards, the British launched a third assault, Cavendish "encouraging his men a fresh with the whole noyse of trumpets." Once more the *Santa Ana* was raked by cannon balls and small shot from the *Desire* and the *Content*, "to the great discomforting of our enemies . . . killing and spoiling many of their men. They being thus discomforted and spoiled, and their shippe being in hazard of sinking by reason of the great shots which were made, whereof some were under water . . ."

At the end of five or six hours of fighting the *Santa Ana* "set out a flagge of truce and parled for mercy, desiring our Generall to save their lives and take their goods, and that they would presently yield . . ."

Cavendish signaled them a promise of mercy and ordered them "to strike sayles, and to hoyse out their boat and to come aboard: which news they were full glad to heare of . . ." The orders were obeyed and one of the chief officers of the *Santa Ana* "came aboard unto our Generall: and falling downe upon his knees, offered to have kissed our Generals feete, and craved mercie: our General most graciously pardoned both him and the rest upon promise of their true dealing with him and his company concerning such riches as were in the shippe . . ."

The captain of the *Santa Ana* presented Cavendish with an inventory of the goods in his cargo, which Pretty recorded as being "an hundredth and 22 thousand pezos of golde . . . silkes, sattens, damasks, with muske & divers other merchandize, and great store of all manner of victuals with the choyse of many conserves of all sortes to eate, and of sundry sortes of very good wines."

The *Santa Ana* was taken into a small harbor near the end of the Baja California peninsula and anchored, "and here the whole company of Spaniards, both of men and women to the number of 190 persons were set on shore: Where they had a fayre river of fresh water, with a great store of fresh fish, foule, and wood, and also many hares . . ." Cavendish, displaying unusual kindness, permitted them to take the *Santa Ana*'s sails for tents and enough planks from the ship to make a small craft in which they could reach safety.

The most valuable goods aboard the *Santa Ana* were removed to the two British ships. After a celebration, Cavendish gave the Spaniards some swords and guns with which to protect themselves from Indians, and ordered the *Santa Ana* fired. On November 19, he set sail for the Philippines, leaving smoke rising from the badly crippled *Santa Ana*.

The *Content* was lost in the Pacific, but Cavendish sailed the *Desire*, carrying a heavy treasure, around the world. He returned to Plymouth in September 1588 and was given a hero's welcome.

Unknown to him, his arsonists had not done a thorough job in setting fire to the *Santa Ana*. A later chronicler would record that after capturing the *Santa Ana* Cavendish "had put the people on shore, and having taken out of the *Santa Ana* what he pleased, he set fire to her and burned her down to the water's edge. As what was left of her unburned remained afloat on the water, the waves carried her into this bay. The Spaniards, who were on land without resource, on seeing this plunged into the sea and boarded her. Throwing out the ballast [remaining cargo and equipment] she carried, they were left with sufficient hulk, which they equipped as best they could with some jury-masts [temporary rigging and the sails given them for tents]. With this they were able to reach Acapulco."

Villamanrique left office in 1590, and another Luis de Velasco became Viceroy of Mexico.* He immediately set in motion programs and policies for the development of the Philippine trade. One of his chief objectives was the discovery of a good harbor on the northwest coast, a project to which Villamanrique had been strongly opposed.

Velasco was capable and energetic, but he was thwarted by the slowness of communications between Mexico City and Spain, by red tape, by a lack of funds, and by a shortage of explorers he considered both competent and worthy of his trust. Three years passed before he had received royal approval of his plan and could act upon it.

Velasco engaged Sebastián Rodríguez Cermeño to make a reconnaissance of the northwest coast on a return trip from the Philippines. Cermeño was a Portuguese, but Velasco in-

---

* Velasco was a son of the former Viceroy with the same name.

formed the King that "he was very skilled in navigation," and moreover, "no Spaniards were available at the moment to make the discovery."

Cermeño had been a pilot on the *Santa Ana* when it was captured by Cavendish. He was not only well informed about navigational problems to be met in the Pacific but fully understood the dangers involved in such a venture, especially those that might be encountered on the return voyage in a vessel loaded with valuable cargo. As extra remuneration for his services he was given permission to bring back in his ship several tons of goods of his own, from which he might derive a profit for himself. He sailed from Acapulco with a flotilla in March 1594. On July 5, 1595, he left the Philippines without escort on his voyage of discovery.

His ship, the *San Augustín*, was of two hundred tons burden, and was heavily loaded with 130 tons of Oriental merchandise, estimated to be worth almost a hundred thousand pesos. Also on board was an unusual cargo. It was a launch which had been constructed in sections. When Cermeño reached the coast of New Spain, the pieces could be fitted and fastened together, and the light craft could be used for examining rivers, bays, and estuaries before taking the ship into them.

After a difficult voyage of four months, Cermeño came in sight of the northwest coast early in November, in the vicinity of Point St. George, almost at the present border between the states of Oregon and California. Bad weather prevented a landing, and for eight or ten days they battled the heavy seas, rain, and adverse winds while working southward along a shore that was "very bold and dangerous because of a heavy surf caused by the many small islands and reefs near land . . ." Suffering greatly on account of the strong gale and the heavy sea, and believing the ship in great danger, several officers made a written demand that Cermeño run with the wind and

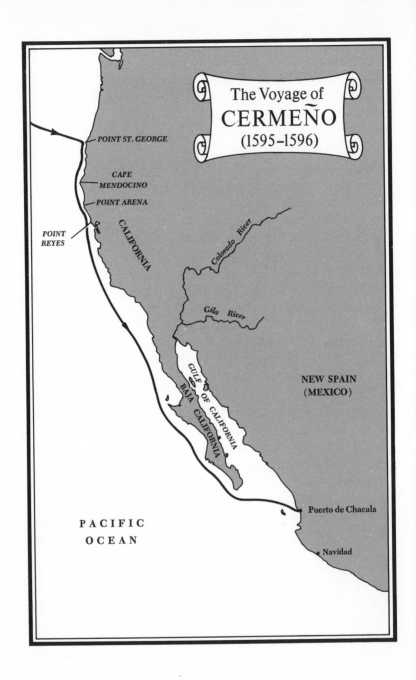

The Voyage of
CERMEÑO
(1595–1596)

POINT ST. GEORGE

CAPE
MENDOCINO

POINT ARENA

POINT
REYES

CALIFORNIA

Colorado River

Gila River

GULF OF CALIFORNIA

BAJA CALIFORNIA

NEW SPAIN
(MEXICO)

Puerto de Chacala

Navidad

PACIFIC
OCEAN

proceed on the voyage to Acapulco "as it was impossible to prosecute the discovery by reason of the ship's being in such a badly battered state . . ." Cermeño rejected the plea, and fortunately the weather improved.

Cape Mendocino and Point Arena were noted and passed, and on a day near the middle of November Point Reyes was turned, and they saw ahead a large *ensenada*, or cove. Sounding their way cautiously into it, they anchored to a bottom that was "clean and of fine sand . . . in five fathoms . . . about a quarter of a league from shore."

They were in the horseshoe-shaped *ensenada* that would come to be known as Drakes Bay, named for the notorious British pilot who may or may not have entered it when he was raiding Spanish ships along the coast seventeen years earlier.

Cermeño ordered the launch put together and lowered into the water. An official report of the voyage, later prepared in Mexico for the Spanish government, relates that on the day the ship anchored, "many Indians appeared on the beach and soon one of them got into a small craft . . . He came off to the ship where he remained quite a time talking in his language, no one understanding what he said. Some cotton cloth and silk things were given him and a red cap. He took them and went back to land."

Had the men on the ship been able to understand the Indian they undoubtedly would have learned of Drake's visit to the vicinity, and perhaps of other Spaniards who had entered the bay. More Indians came out to the ship the following morning, and after giving them presents Cermeño disembarked in the launch ". . . with twenty-two men, seventeen being harquebusiers with their arms . . . They went ashore with the Indians and landed on the beach near some of their underground habitations, in which they live . . ." These people may have belonged to the division of the Moquelumnan linguistic family, who dwelt along the coast between the Golden Gate and Bodega Bay. The official report described them as "well-made, robust and more corpulent than the Spaniards in general. They go naked without covering and with their private parts exposed, but the women cover theirs with straw and skins of animals. Their arms are bows and arrows. They wear their hair long and have no beards. They are painted on the breast and certain parts of the arms . . . They were all very peaceable . . . They produce a seed the shape of an anise seed, only a little thinner, and having the taste of sesame, of which they make the bread they eat. Their food consists of crabs and wild birds, which are in great abundance near where they live, and many deer . . ."

With solemn ceremony, Cermeño "took possession of the land and the port in the name of the King, our master. He gave it the name La Baya de San Francisco, and the Reverend Father Fray Francisco de la Concepción of the Order of the Barefoot Franciscans, who comes in the ship, baptized it."

As Cermeño and his company were ready to return to the ship, another band of Indians "approached in a warlike manner, for as soon as they saw the Spaniards they performed a caracole and skirmished in a circle . . . with loud howls. Shortly, one of them who carried a tall banner of black feathers began to advance towards where the Spaniards were . . . Two Indians, of the friendly ones who were being treated well, talked with them and soon they lowered their arms, put them on the ground, and came toward the Spaniards. The one who carried the banner brought and delivered it to the Captain and all the other Indians approached in an humble manner as if terrorized, and yielded peacefully." Cermeño embraced them and gave them gifts of the sashes worn by his men. These Indians "had their faces painted and anointed in black and red." It seemed apparent that they belonged to another tribe which lived farther inland, and had come to the coast either to gather seafood or to visit their neighbors, the Moquelumnans.

Cermeño had elected to establish a camp on the beach, and although all the Indians indicated a wish to remain on friendly terms, he took no chances. He ordered an entrenchment built and maintained a guard throughout the night. On the next day, November 15, he set out on the first of a number of excursions to examine the bay and the surrounding country. It was during the course of these explorations, which were continued for several days, that his expedition was brought to a tragic end.

The *San Augustín* was anchored west of the Drake Estero in Drakes Bay, a location which left it exposed to any turbulence that might approach from the south. Why Cermeño, a veteran navigator, had chosen the site was not adequately explained. He may have considered it safe enough in the belief that storms in the area came from the north, as it was known that the prevailing winds blew from that direction.

Whatever the case, a furious winter gale swept in from the south. The *San Augustín* was driven on the rocks and completely destroyed, its valuable cargo and all supplies being scattered over the normally peaceful waters of Drakes Bay.

Twelve men perished in the wreck. The survivors, numbering "more than seventy," faced a desperate situation. They had only a small amount of food supplies, few arms, and their only means of escape was the open launch. They were able during the next few days to obtain some acorns, wild fruit, and dried meat from the Indians for the voyage to Mexico, and "on Friday morning, December 8 . . . Captain Sebastián Rodríguez [Cermeño] departed from the Puerto y Bahía de San Francisco . . . in the launch . . . named the *San Buenaventura* . . ."

Cermeno's ship, the San Augustín, was driven on the rocks and its cargo strewn over Drakes Bay.

The name of the launch was inappropriate, for the voyage was anything but a *good venture*. Taking advantage of favorable weather, they pushed southward as rapidly as possible, sometimes sailing throughout the night. At one place they ran so closely along the California coast "that many people could be seen on shore on some cliffs, where they had their huts. Near sundown he anchored in front of some villages . . . He spoke to them, shouting out from the launch that we were Christians. One of them responded and said 'Christianos,' and at once came running down to the shore, and taking a *balsa* [canoe] and getting into it came alongside the launch . . ." The Indian was given pieces of cloth, and "shortly many other Indians came out . . . and were asked by signs to bring some food . . . They went ashore and very soon came back bringing a quantity of bitter acorns and some corn mush . . ." These were Indians whom Unamuno had met, but now they were "quiet and peaceable . . . and exclaimed 'Mexico, Mexico' "—to show they previously had talked with Spaniards.

On some days heavy surf made a landing impossible, and the men were weak and sick from terrible hunger. On some days they were sustained by nothing more than some shellfish or some acorns. Once "the men killed a dog on the launch and ate it"—how the animal was obtained was not explained.

They stopped in a cove of San Miguel Island, on which Cabrillo had met with his fatal accident, but they were able to obtain from Indians only twelve fish and a small seal . . . hardly enough to have any effect on the maddening hunger of so many men. They caught thirty more fish by hook and line, and then sailed on along the coast.

The next day some of the men were able to reach an Indian village on another island after fighting their way ashore through heavy surf, and they "brought back some cakes made of a very yellow root resembling the sweet potato, which are

cooked under the sand. This made some of those who ate
them very sick." In another place "where some Spaniards
went ashore many wild onions and tunas were found, and near
the water among the rocks a very large fish which had been
killed with two wounds. On this more than seventy people
sustained themselves for eight days, and if it had not been for
this fish all the men, in view of their conditions, ran much risk
of losing their lives." Obtaining sufficient fresh water was a
constant problem, and there were days and nights when the
men were half-crazed from thirst.

Miraculously, on January 7, 1596, thirty days after leaving
Drakes Bay, the coast of Compostela, Mexico, came in sight of
the suffering men in the *San Buenaventura*, almost all of
whom were near death from malnutrition and disease. A landing was made "a league from the Puerto de Chacala, where
from a ranch some corn and sun-dried beef was brought to aid
them . . ."

If Viceroy Velasco needed another argument in favor of establishing a base on the northwest coast, he had it.

If it accomplished nothing else, the disastrous voyage of Cermeño changed the thinking of Spanish officials. A new policy
was adopted, in the conviction that no satisfactory results
could be obtained by sending loaded ships returning from the
Philippines to search for a port on the far northern coast.

Velasco proposed that a flotilla of small vessels, carrying no
cargo, be sent on the important mission from Acapulco. After
considering the matter, the Council of the Indies decided that
government interests would be best served by sending only a
single vessel, and Velasco was bound by this ruling. Before an
expedition could be organized, however, the decision would be
rescinded, and when the exploration finally was undertaken,
three vessels would participate.

Now a man came upon the scene who was to play a starring role in the history of California for several years. He was Sebastián Vizcaíno, a Basque, who had arrived in Mexico about 1585. He married a woman of property, but he apparently had made considerable money in business himself, although at the time he came into prominence he was no more than thirty-five years of age.

Vizcaíno was both a competent trader and a shrewd promoter. He quickly became interested in the Philippine trade, and had not been long in Mexico before he set sail for the far-off islands. Unfortunately for him, he was returning on the *Santa Ana* when it was taken by Cavendish. He claimed to have suffered a heavy personal loss in "treasure and commodities" he had been bringing back to Mexico in the galleon. Soon he made another trip to Manila, which apparently brought him profit.

Vizcaíno next turned his attention to promoting a pearl-fishing expedition to Baja California. He obtained a contract from Viceroy Velasco, but several of his partners defaulted in this agreement and were brought before a criminal court. In 1595 Velasco awarded Vizcaíno a new contract. Under its provisions, besides establishing a pearl fishery, he was to found a settlement at the southern end of the Baja California peninsula. He organized an expedition.

Meanwhile, a new Viceroy had taken office in Mexico. He was Don Gaspar de Zúñiga y Azevedo, Count of Monterey, and he viewed Vizcaíno's enterprise with disfavor. Vizcaíno, he wrote the King, "was lacking in character, resolution and capacity," and he feared that to trust such an important project to him might result in mistreatment of the Indians. The Council of the Indies agreed, and the Count of Monterey was authorized to appoint someone else to command the undertaking. Before he could take action, Vizcaíno had sailed from

Acapulco with three ships carrying "230 seamen and soldiers and men and women colonists, fourteen horses, arms, ammunition and supplies for them, twelve pieces of small artillery and food for eight months."

The project was a fiasco. Neither a pearl fishery nor a settlement was established, although a town was laid out and given the name of La Paz. The sailors and soldiers got into fights with the Indians. No food supplies could be obtained in the barren country. Nineteen men were drowned when a ship's boat upset during a landing. The camp, the supplies, and most of the munitions and weapons were destroyed in a fire. By the beginning of the year 1597, Vizcaíno and all the others, most of them sick and dispirited, were back in Mexico.

Undaunted, Vizcaíno set out to organize another pearl-fishing venture, and sought a government loan. The Count of Monterey had other ideas. He wanted to give a friend, Gabriel Maldonado, a chance to discover the rich pearl beds that were believed to exist along the Baja California peninsula. Maldonado, who had influential political friends in Spain, was an experienced pearl hunter, having been in the business in other waters for ten years. There was, however, a stumbling block. Vizcaíno still had a legal contract to search for pearls in the Gulf of California, and the Viceroy admitted that it would be unjust to cancel it arbitrarily "after Vizcaíno and his partners had spent so much money." He expressed the belief that Vizcaíno had "displayed some moderate talent and more spirit than could be ordinarily expected from a merchant," and he attributed Vizcaíno's failure chiefly to "ignorance of the seas, and to having undertaken the journey without having given proper thought to the burden of the ships, and with an unnecessary number of men and an insufficient supply of certain kinds of food."

In view of what the Count of Monterey had in mind, this

was hardly an appropriate statement, but it seemed to have the desired effect. He had in mind purchasing Vizcaíno's ships, and naming Vizcaíno to command an expedition to explore the northwest coast. The plan would clear the way for Maldonado to search for pearls in the Gulf of California.

King Philip II of Spain died in the fall of 1598. His son, Philip III, ascended to the throne. A year passed before the new King approved the Count of Monterey's proposal, and authorized him to place Vizcaíno in command of the projected voyage of exploration.

The Count of Monterey ordered the expedition to be prepared and to start as early as possible in 1601. Vizcaíno was instructed to examine the northwest coast in great detail, "make soundings in the ports and ascertain their landmarks, take the sun every day and the north star every night, search the ports for pearls, and make maps of the discoveries."

Although Vizcaíno would be the nominal commander, or general, the Viceroy's confidence in him was limited, so he appointed a council "of reputable, experienced naval, military and religious men" to sail with him. Vizcaíno was to do nothing of importance without the approval of a majority of the councilors, and was not permitted to cast a vote except in case of a tie.

Considerable difficulties in equipping the ships and enlisting sailors, soldiers, and officers were encountered. The scheduled departure time in 1601 passed, and preparations had not been completed. Advised that it would be disadvantageous to begin the vital exploration late in the year, when the worst storms occurred in the North Pacific, the Count of Monterey ordered the voyage postponed until the following spring.

Two vessels were ready to leave in March, but the third, coming to join them in Acapulco from another port, was damaged en route and had to undergo repairs.

At last, on Sunday, May 5, 1602, a piece of artillery was discharged as a signal to weigh anchors, and the three vessels, the *San Diego*, the *Santo Tomás* and the *Tres Reyes*, spread their sails to the warm tropical breeze and left the harbor of Acapulco.

6

The Neglected Land

VIZCAÍNO'S FLAGSHIP WAS THE two-hundred-ton *San Diego*. The *Santo Tomás* was perhaps half its size, and the *Tres Reyes* was an open *fragata*, probably of no more than forty tons burden. Crowded aboard the three vessels were more than two hundred men. Besides the usual complements of sailors, soldiers, pilots, and officers, there were cosmographers, cartographers, military and naval advisers, and highly educated men of the Church. The company might well be termed the first scientific expedition to the land of California.

One of the most learned members was Fray Antonio de la Ascensión of the Barefoot Order of Nuestra Señora del Carmel. Father Ascensión, a noted cosmographer, a student of natural history, an expert navigator, and a distinguished religious leader, was the chief chronicler of the great voyage. He left to posterity invaluable descriptions of Indians, animals, fish, and birds, and he drew charts and scientifically recorded the topography of the Pacific coast. It might be said that he was the first true California "booster," for he fell in love with the country, ecstatically praised its beauty, and repeatedly expressed the conviction that it contained great treasures of gold and other precious metals.

Their course lay up the coast of Mexico as far as Mazatlán, where they replenished their supplies of wood and water, and then across the Gulf of California, almost on the Tropic of Cancer. This part of the journey consumed a month. "Our Lord was pleased," wrote Father Ascensión, "that on Sunday afternoon, June 9, the fleet should come in sight of the Californias. Approaching the Cabo de San Lucas [at the southern tip of the Baja California Peninsula] in order to search for a port there, the fog came up so thick and dark that the ships became separated. Losing contact with each other and without knowing where the others were, they went on for a day and a half."

Before the exploration of the California coast had begun, a serious disaster was narrowly avoided, and Father Ascensión recorded that "it was a recognized miracle of God that the *Santo Tomás* [in which he was at the time a passenger] was not wrecked on some reefs of this cape. As in the darkness she was just about to strike them, not being fifty paces from them, the fog cleared up for just a moment, and thus the danger was seen." The seamen had just enough time "to put the helm to the side, and with this the ship came up with her bow to the sea. It was a miraculous thing, because in an instant the day darkened again with the fog as heavy and thick as before." Later the day cleared and the vessels took refuge "in a good bay near the cape."

The first landing in Baja California was made, ". . . and on the beach a great quantity of fresh sardines was found which had been left there by the return of the waves. These in endeavoring to escape from other larger fish had come close to shore and the waves had thrown them out and left them dry. So many and so good were they that on what was collected all

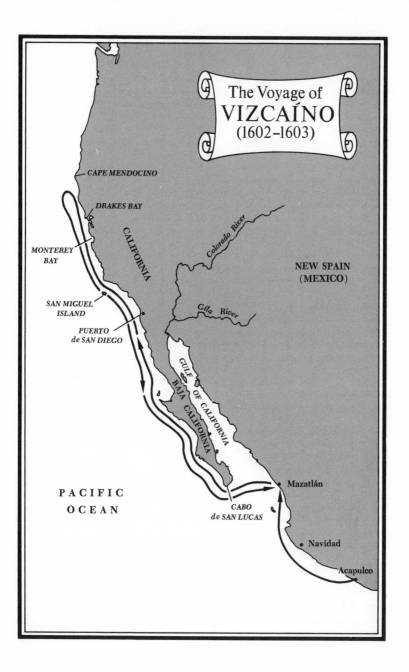

The Voyage of **VIZCAÍNO** (1602–1603)

CAPE MENDOCINO

DRAKES BAY

MONTEREY BAY

CALIFORNIA

SAN MIGUEL ISLAND

PUERTO de SAN DIEGO

Colorado River

Gila River

NEW SPAIN (MEXICO)

GULF OF CALIFORNIA

BAJA CALIFORNIA

PACIFIC OCEAN

Mazatlán

CABO de SAN LUCAS

Navidad

Acapulco

those of the fleet supped that night and dined the following day. On the beach were found many heaps of mother-of-pearl shells in which pearls grow. There were many of these shells scattered through the sand, which, struck by the rays of the sun at midday, scintillated like stars, making it look like a starry heaven. From this the great richness of pearls in that sea can be readily seen. It is certain they are there and very fine ones at that."

Progress was slow as they worked their way northward in the Pacific from Cabo de San Lucas, for they carefully examined the coast, took soundings, charted the topography, made many landings, and took many observations. It was not until early November, six months after they had left Acapulco, that they passed north of the future borderline between Mexico and American California.

"Little by little," said Father Ascensión, "they made their voyage, coasting along the land, on all of which many fires and smokes were seen by day and by night. These the Indians made, as if calling to the ships to come close to their country, which showed indications of being good, fertile and level and was of pleasing aspect."

On November 10, 1602, they entered a bay which they named Puerto de San Diego, "a port very capacious, good, large and safe, as it was protected from all winds."

Sixty years earlier, Cabrillo had made an almost identical report. A tempest had struck while he was anchored in San Diego Bay (to which he had given another name), but his ships had suffered no damage. Father Ascensión made no mention of Cabrillo.

With warm fall weather prevailing, Vizcaíno decided to rest for a time in the pleasant surroundings, clean and repair the ships, and take on wood and water. He "ordered a spacious tent to be set up on shore to serve as a church where the friars could say mass every day they were there." It is believed that these were the first full religious services before a properly adorned altar to be conducted in American California.

The bountiful natural resources of the country made a profound impression on Father Ascensión. He spoke of its great fertility, of its trees and grasslands. The Indians brought the Spaniards "fine skins of martens, cats, seals and other animals, net bags and little nets with which they fished." The waters gave up a rich harvest of "white fish called smelts, skates, oysters, mussels, sardines, lobsters . . . and there are many white and brown geese, ducks, quail, hares, and rabbits." On one beach "there was a great quantity of sparkling golden pyrites," which he considered "a sure sign that there must be gold mines in the mountains." On a sandbar "there were some great large pieces like cow dung, very light in weight . . . some said they were pieces of amber."

On the maps prepared by the Vizcaíno expedition were written many place names still in use today, such as San Diego, San Pedro, the names of some of the islands off the southern California coast, the Santa Barbara Channel, Carmel, and numerous others. In mid-December they gave the name of Santa Lucia to mountains capped with snow, and on December 16 entered a large bay, which they christened Monterey in honor of the Viceroy of New Spain.

Monterey Bay seemed to Vizcaíno, Father Ascensión and others an ideal place to establish a colony and a haven for the homebound galleons from the Orient. "Those who come from China," said Father Ascensión, "could very well resort to this port. It is in the same region and parallel of latitude as Seville, and is almost of the same climate. The Spaniards could settle here as an assistance to those sailing from China, as it is of the climate and quality of our Spain . . . It is a very good port and well protected from all winds. There is much wood and

Father Ascención praised the natural beauty of Monterey Bay.

water in it and an immense number of great pine trees, smooth and straight, suitable for the masts and yards of ships; many very large live-oaks with which to build ships . . . There are rock-roses, broom, roses of Castile . . . beautiful large lakes, which were covered with ducks and many other birds; most fertile pastures; good meadows for cattle, and fertile fields for growing crops. There are many different kinds of animals . . . large bears, lions, elk, deer, stags, rabbits, geese, doves, quail, partridges . . . many good fish . . . oysters, lobsters, crabs . . . many large seals and whales."

Interwoven into Father Ascensión's account of the natural beauty, the richness and bountifulness of California, is a tragic tale of terrible illness and death. Even before the ships had departed from San Diego, scurvy had begun to take a toll of the men. With all the fish and meat and starchy food that was available to them, they were succumbing to the great scourge of the sea, the frightful disease caused by a deficiency of ascorbic acid, now identified as vitamin C, obtained from fruits and leafy vegetables, and so vital to good health.

By the time Monterey had been reached, sixteen men had been buried at sea, and "there was now scarcely one who could say he was entirely sound and perfectly well . . . there were deaths each day . . . The sensitiveness of the bodies of these sick people is so great that the very clothing put on them is felt like sharp darts or cruel lances . . . they emit cries so pitiful that they reach the heavens . . . this sickness and pestilential humour brings on other results more insufferable and loathsome . . . the upper and lower gums become swollen . . . the teeth become so loose and without support that they move." Victims "spat out unexpectedly a couple of teeth at a time." The disease also "attacks the back and the kidneys so that one cannot move . . . there is no consolation except to ask God to help one or take one away from this life."

After a lengthy consideration of the desperate situation, Vizcaíno and the council decided to send the *Santo Tomás* back to Acapulco with the sick. The *San Diego* and the *Tres Reyes* would go on with the "rest of the men who were well and with some strength," and attempt to carry out the Viceroy's order to explore the coast at least as far north as Cape Mendocino.

Copies of reports and maps were prepared for the Count of Monterey, and on December 29 the *Santo Tomás* sailed southward with its pitiful cargo. More than forty sailors, soldiers, and officers had died, and more would succumb, but Father Ascensión believed that "Our Lord, Jesus Christ, was pleased that all passed away after having been confessed and received extreme unction," and "having made their wills, arranged for the welfare of their souls and discharged their consciences."

On January 3, 1603, the *San Diego* and the *Tres Reyes* left Monterey on a disastrous voyage to the north.

Winter storms struck, and the ships became separated. Vizcaíno in the *San Diego* stopped at Puerto de San Francisco (Drakes Bay), but "because of anxiety about the *Tres Reyes*, no men were landed, and in consequence the *San Diego* sailed out on the following day . . . to search for her."

But the *Tres Reyes* was not found. When, on January 13, the *San Diego* was in sight of Cape Mendocino, ". . . a southeast wind came up with the greatest fury and with it a fog or mist so cold and dark that the day seemed like night. The sea became so wild that it seemed that with each wave the ship would be lost or submerged."

Vizcaíno and the council agreed that they had gone far enough, for ". . . there were not six men on board all told who were well and up, the rest of the soldiers, sailors, cabin boys, and ship boys being sick in bed with the same disease

. . . Not only were these in their beds, but also the friars and the captain-counsellors. They were so sick and spent that Father Andrés (who was the least sick) could scarcely come to confess and anoint those who were dying." Father Ascensión was unable to move from his own bed.

On January 14 the storm abated for a brief time, and the *San Diego* was turned homeward. But another tempest struck on the following day, and until the 19th the ship rolled helplessly with all sails furled. Then "the wind changed and commenced to blow from the northwest. With this the day cleared up . . ." The *San Diego* ran southward before it.

A ship of living death, the *San Diego* reached Mazatlán on February 17. Only five men on board had the strength to handle the sails and steer. Miraculously, within three weeks the health of all was restored.

The cure came, as Father Ascensión recounted, "not by doctors or surgeons, medicines or other drugs from the pharmacies, nor by any human remedy . . ." It came from "papayas, bananas, oranges, lemons, pumpkins, and *quiletes* [a vegetable eaten as greens]." The edible fruit of a cactus, which Father Ascensión called *manzanillas*, was particularly beneficial, truly the wonder drug of the day, for after the sufferer had eaten it only a few times, pain vanished, gums and teeth hardened, and strength returned.

In March the *San Diego*, manned by healthy sailors, left for Acapulco, arriving on the 19th. There it was reunited with the long lost *Tres Reyes*, whose men had fared no better than those of the *San Diego*. Each ship had searched for the other after they had become separated in the vicinity of Cape Mendocino. At last each had turned back for Mexico. When the *San Diego* was anchored at Mazatlán, the *Tres Reyes* had passed by, and had gone on to Navidad. Sailing to Acapulco, the *San Diego* had passed by Navidad, where the *Tres Reyes* was at anchor. Thus, the two ships had narrowly missed a re-union before reaching Acapulco.

Father Ascensión apparently was not well informed about the discoveries of Alarcón and Melchior Díaz, who had learned that the Gulf of California ended where the Colorado River entered it, and, therefore, the peninsula of Baja California was not an island. Nor, apparently, had he read the reports of Cabrillo and other voyagers along the northwest coast. For he expressed the belief "that the whole Kingdom of California discovered on this voyage, is the largest island known . . . it is separated from the provinces of New Mexico by the Mediterranean Sea of California, which some call the 'Mar de Cortez' because he was the first to discover it . . ." Father Ascensión's conviction that California was surrounded by water long continued to be shared by many other men, and it was shown as an island on maps for years to come.

Father Ascensión saw California as a "promised land," declaring with some sternness that "in justice and charity" the Spanish King was under obligation to colonize it. "The grandeur, length and width of the Kingdom of California," he wrote, "the many people there, and their docility, make it easy to teach them the mysteries of our Holy Catholic faith . . . The great riches it promises in pearls, gold, silver, and amber . . . have been observed. None of this can be enjoyed if the affairs of that kingdom remain in the state in which we found them, and the great expenses which have been incurred will come to naught, unless His Majesty endeavors to pacify, conquer, and settle it with Spaniards."

He recommended that the first settlement be made at the southern end of the Baja California peninsula (the beginning of the "island"). If a good city was established in this location, other colonies could be built at suitable places to the north, "and all this great kingdom can be pacified very peaceably in a very short time . . ." Not only would large numbers of heathens be brought under the banners of Christianity, but the trade from the Orient would greatly benefit. From the northern coast of California "an entrance can be made to the Kingdom of Anian, and from there to Great China, the Great Tartary . . . Thus His Majesty could come with great ease to be king and supreme emperor of all the world with a good and quiet conscience . . ."

Confused geography blended with great dreams. What happened was quite different from what Father Ascensión envisioned.

Vizcaíno began a campaign to have Monterey developed as a port and a Spanish colony, and for a time it appeared that he would meet with success. In letters to the King and the Viceroy he stressed the good qualities of Monterey Harbor, and offered to "dedicate himself and what remained of his property and health to the task of settling it." Nor did he neglect to mention that numerous persons, himself among them, were of the opinion that valuable metals were to be found in the adjacent country. Certain mountains had shown signs of containing gold.

The Count of Monterey was convinced that Vizcaíno's judgment was sound. If a colony was to be established on the northwest coast, Monterey appeared to be the best location for it. He recommended that "Vizcaíno and the private persons who went with him on his voyage of discovery should be honored and rewarded." However, the Count of Monterey ultimately would reveal that he possessed strong reservations regarding the wisdom and feasibility of the project.

Vizcaíno petitioned the Court of Mexico to hear sworn testimony from himself and witnesses regarding the value of his services to his country and the personal expenses he had incurred during his explorations. His purpose was to place this evidence on record, after which he would request of His Majesty an official appointment to high office and a grant of lands which would bring him an assured annual income. It was clear that Vizcaíno hoped to become governor of the new California colony and to make a fortune from its resources.

After hearings the Court certified its view that Vizcaíno had rendered valuable services to the government and merited a reward from the King. Political reassignments, however, disrupted the smooth process of the case. In 1603 the Count of Monterey was transferred to the government of Peru, and Juan de Mendoza y Luna, the Marqués de Montesclaros, was made Viceroy of Mexico.

Vizcaíno had been named to command a fleet sailing for the Philippines. He was to return with a number of navigators to Monterey to instruct them in the route and familiarize them with the new port. Viceroy Mendoza removed him, gave the command to an old friend, and appointed Vizcaíno *alcalde* of Tehauntepec.

For three years the issue dragged slowly through the red tape that clogged official channels. In 1606 the Council of the Indies recommended that Vizcaíno should be appointed to establish a settlement at Monterey, and that money should be appropriated from the royal treasury for the purpose.

King Philip III reprimanded the Viceroy for removing Vizcaíno, and wrote him: "It has seemed advisable to me that all the ships coming from the Philippines should enter this port [of Monterey], as they sight that coast, and therefore should make repairs and obtain supplies there." The Viceroy was ordered to restore Vizcaíno to command, "honoring him and helping him for the purpose from my royal treasury with what seems proper to you and telling him on my part how much he would serve me in this, and that I shall take care to reward him and remunerate his services . . . In order that his departure on this business can take place soon, I have agreed to order you to dispatch the ships which are to go to the Philippines in the coming year 1607 . . . without paying any attention to any other considerations except my absolute service, as I am confident you will do, so that on the return voyage . . . they can examine the method in which the port of Monterey should be settled . . ."

The King, however, left an escape hatch in his orders, and Viceroy Mendoza did not overlook it. "I therefore shall consider myself served," wrote His Majesty, "if you will commit the settlement to Sebastián Vizcaíno *provided no considerable inconveniences to doing so present themselves to you* . . ." (Italics added.)

Mendoza could cite several "inconveniences" as reasons for not fulfilling the King's orders. One was that when he received them, the ships Vizcaíno was to have commanded had already sailed for Manila. Another was that Vizcaíno had left for Spain to press his own case.

But Mendoza also harbored personal objections to the proposed settlement at Monterey, and he was in a good position to state them bluntly to the King. He had been appointed Viceroy of Peru, and would soon depart, so the whole problem would be transferred to the shoulders of his successor. But although he was on the verge of leaving Mexico, Viceroy Mendoza did not hesitate to unburden himself about an issue which, properly speaking, was no longer his business, and his letters to the King had a significant effect on the course of California history.

Mendoza brought to the attention of the King and the Council of the Indies two islands believed to be located on the return route from the Philippines. Rumors of the existence of these small bodies of land, called Rica de Oro and Rica de

Plata, had circulated for years, and they were reputed to be rich in gold and silver. How the tales about them originated is not certain, but some highly imaginative spinners of yarns, perhaps early Portuguese navigators in the Pacific, had claimed to have sighted them, and they were arbitrarily placed on some charts by credulous cartographers.

In 1584 Gali had told of hearing about them from a Chinese pilot from Changchow, and he had even claimed to have found them. Wrote Gali: "According to the information which the man from Chang-chow gave, I should find after traveling 700 leagues from here [Philippines] four islands not far from one another, which he said he knew because he had seen in Japan some small, broad-shouldered men with big hair-rolls on their heads; the articles they brought with them to be sold were gold in powder and cotton stuff and salted fish like tunny; and they said they came from some islands situated to the east of Japan . . . I found them not far from the place which the Chinese pilot had indicated." This was a pure fabrication, for Gali was unable to give any description of the islands, but his report excited the world, and especially the Spanish.

Three years later, in 1587, Unamuno, sailing from Macao to the northwest coast of New Spain, had searched for the two rich islands. "On July 28," he wrote, "we stood away that same night for the Isla de Oro . . . Its southern part is in 29° and its northern in scant 32½°, according to its position shown on some charts. We found ourselves in this latitude Wednesday, August 19, and searched for the island from east to west and in every other requisite direction. As we did everything possible and could not find it, it may be concluded that it does not exist.

"From this latitude of 31°, we stood away on a east-northeast course for another island, shown on some charts, named Rica de Plata, sixty leagues distant from the one named Rica de Oro and its latitude . . . Here we found ourselves on Saturday, August 22, and although we searched from east to west, making every possible effort, we could not find the island. Doubtless it does not exist, but somebody on hearsay ordered it drawn on his [own] chart."

Unamuno was right. The islands did not exist. But no one in Mexico or Spain would believe that, any more than they would believe that the Strait of Anian did not exist, that more fabulous fortunes in gold and jewels were not awaiting discovery in lands of the New World, that the northwest coast of New Spain did not go on to China, or that, despite the voyages made along both of its coasts, California was not an island.

If His Majesty desired a colony and port for the relief of homebound Manila galleons, Viceroy Mendoza wrote the King, it should be remembered "that in 34° to 35° there are two islands called Rica de Oro and Rica de Plata, directly west of the port of Monterey, almost on the same parallel but at a great distance of longitude. These islands . . . are the ones which all those who have treated about this navigation and have followed it say that it would be convenient to examine and settle in order that the ships may stop there."

The Viceroy Mendoza could hardly have been unaware that there were great doubts the islands existed, for no Spanish navigator had been able to find them. Yet he injected the matter into the controversy for what it was worth. Then he proceeded to advance a truly powerful argument against establishing a colony at Monterey. It was both a contention and a warning forcefully illustrating his hardheadedness, his shrewdness, and his desire to serve his country to the best of his ability. Building a settlement at Monterey, or at some other place on the northwest coast, he declared, might well open the gate to invasion by such powers as the British or the Dutch.

This warning had been sounded twenty years earlier by a previous Viceroy, the Marqués de Villamanrique, but another King had been on the Spanish throne then, and in the passage of two decades it undoubtedly had been forgotten. In reviving it, Mendoza gave it the sound of a dire prediction, writing young King Philip III: "The greatest security and strength in these kingdoms on the coast of your Majesty in the South Sea lie in the difficulty of enemies coming to it and the little assistance they would have in the ports even when in it. In order to do away with this inconvenience, they [foreign explorers] have always been hunting for new ways, always looking for a strait or passage above Cabo Mendocino or by the opening of the Californias. It seemed to them that the day they should find it they would have secured with little effort what would be the best for them."

He pleaded with the King to ask himself what would happen if Spain should aid other powers by colonizing the northwest coast. If Spain's enemies should gain this advantage, "it is easy to see how risky everything would be and how necessary it would be that each merchant ship that went to the Philippines should have two armed ships to protect the passage, with extraordinary expense and perpetual alarm on the coasts of Peru and New Spain."

Mendoza thought this surely would be the result of building a port "in a place which is not necessary," and he begged the King "to order this looked into again as there is time before putting it into execution."

Mendoza went on to Peru, and for a second time Luis de Velasco, the younger, became Viceroy of Mexico. Although Velasco had long favored settling the northwest coast, the problem was already out of his hands. Mendoza's arguments had been placed before the Council of the Indies, and it began deliberations on the question late in 1607.

The Council moved slowly, but at last resolved to recommend that, in view of Mendoza's objections, the King send an order to Viceroy Velasco to do nothing more about a port at Monterey until the islands of Rica de Oro and Rica de Plata had been discovered and examined. If the islands were found to be suitable, declared the Council, they, not Monterey, should be settled. The Council also recommended that Vizcaíno be placed in command of the ships which would be sent to find the islands.

The King heeded the advice of the Council. In September 1608, Viceroy Velasco received orders to withhold all further consideration of Monterey as a haven on the Manila-Acapulco route.

Three more years passed before Vizcaíno was sent out to search for the islands. Needless to say, he did not find them.

If not forgotten, California became a neglected land. More than a hundred and fifty years would pass before Spain once more took action to establish settlements on the northwest coast and build bases at San Diego and Monterey.

During this long period, no more exploring expeditions were sent by sea northward from Mexico. The Spanish galleons continued to bring their rich cargoes from the Orient. Few of them sighted the California coast. Almost invariably they took a course to the southeast while still several hundred miles west of Monterey, and pointed as directly as possible toward Acapulco. Pirates captured some of them, but losses were not excessive. The Philippine trade was highly profitable.

Some of the world's greatest silver mines were developed in central and northern Mexico. The mission frontier was pushed steadily northward, and church bells pealed in arid, barren Baja California. New Mexico was colonized, and Santa Fe and Albuquerque and other settlements were founded. Daring priests who would have welcomed martyrdom went far into the wilderness to carry the banners of Christianity among the Indians. Between 1687 and 1710, the famed missionary-explorer, Father Eusebio Kino, opened trails across the deserts of the Southwest, founded the first cattle and sheep ranches, and built the first missions in the land that would become Arizona. He drew accurate maps of the country at the head of the Gulf of California, and proposed a geographical division of the vast land, so much of it still unknown, that Cortez, Ulloa, Alarcón, Cabrillo, and others had discovered. The southern part he called Baja California, the northern part Alta California, and the borderline he drew between the two regions was virtually where it remains today.

By the late 1760's, the necessity of protecting its Pacific frontiers at last forced Spain to give serious thought once more to building military and naval bases on the coast of Alta California. Events of great significance had occurred, which dramatically portended the shape of things to come.

Great Britain had become the world's most powerful and far-flung nation. The saying that the sun never set on the British Empire was literally true, for its colonies encircled the globe. British explorers (as well as buccaneers) were in every part of the Pacific, and there were well-founded reports that Britain was planning to gain a monopoly of the oceanic trade not only in Oriental and Australian waters but along the western coast of North America, and especially the northern part of it. England already had thirteen flourishing colonies spread along the Atlantic seaboard.

In the Seven Years' War,* the French were defeated in Canada, and Spain, allied with the French, lost Cuba and the

---

* 1756–1763. Known in America as the French and Indian War.

Philippines to the British. To compensate Spain for these losses, France, anxious to end the disastrous conflict, secretly ceded to Spain all its possessions west of the Mississippi—the gigantic region called Louisiana.

Under the terms of the Treaty of Paris, negotiated in 1763, France yielded to England all of Canada and the port of Mobile, on the Gulf of Mexico. Cuba and the Philippines were restored to Spain, but in exchange for these concessions Spain was forced to cede to Great Britain all her possessions east of the Mississippi, which included East and West Florida.

British explorers were continuing to search for a Northwest Passage between the Atlantic and the Pacific, but whether they ever found it or not, England was now in a position to move overland from Canada westward to the coast.

Spain viewed as another serious threat to its northwest frontier the activities of the Russians. They had been for some years engaged in fur trade in Alaska, which they had discovered, and reports reached the Spanish government that Catherine the Great intended to establish a Russian colony in California.

Thus, in 1768 Spain saw itself in a position where it had no alternative but to undertake the colonization of California, if it were to protect its Pacific frontier against the schemes of the British and the Russians. José de Gálvez, the King's special representative in Mexico, was ordered to take immediate steps to organize the conquest.

Gálvez wasted no time. The maps drawn by Father Ascensión and other men with the Vizcaíno voyage of 1603 were resurrected from the archives, where they had lain for more than a hundred and fifty years. Gálvez's plans were comprehensive and carefully drawn. They called for two expeditions, one by land and one by sea. He was taking no chances of meeting with failure. As Vizcaíno had advocated so long before,

Spanish missions were not established in California until late in the eighteenth century.

Monterey was selected as the site of the main presidio, but settlements would be established as well in other feasible locations, so that the whole coast might be protected against foreign invaders. Religious considerations were not overlooked. With the settlers and soldiers would go a contingent of Franciscan friars led by Father Junipero Serra, who became the founder of the twenty-one missions that eventually were built in California.

On April 11, 1769, the packet *San Antonio* entered San Diego Bay. A few days later a sister ship, the *San Carlos*, came in. The sea expedition was joined by the first of two land contingents in May, and the next month the remainder of the land forces arrived.

The settlement of California had begun—229 years after the first Spaniards had set foot on its earth.